Allies at Work

Allies at Work

Creating a Lesbian, Gay, Bisexual and Transgender Inclusive Work Environment

David M. Hall, Ed.D.

Library of Congress
Hall, David.
  Allies at work: creating a lesbian, gay, bisexual and transgender
inclusive work environment / David M. Hall.
p. cm.
Includes bibliographical references and index.
ISBN 978-0-615-30682-7 (hardcover: alk. paper)
1. Corporate culture 2. Diversity and inclusion I. Title
HD58.7.H38 2009

Printed in the United States of America
FIRST EDITION
HB Printing

This book is dedicated
in loving memory
to my mother, Debby Hall,
who was everyone's ally

Contents

Allies at Work

ACKNOWLEDGMENTS

While only the author's name appears on the cover of a book, there are a number of people, my allies, who have been essential to this work reaching publication.

While these individuals were not directly involved with this book, they have been a personal inspiration and have shaped my work: Dr. Don Dyson, Leash Fasciocco, Victoria Fuller, Richard George, Alexis Gordon, Eli Green, Bradley Giuranna, Teresa Greisemer, Burt Hynes, Juliann Labor, Dr. Konnie McCaffree, Brent Reinhard, Dr. Brent Satterly, Beth Soderberg, Michael Soileau, Joelle Townsend, David Trevaskis, Esq., and Phillip Wellbank. After recognizing the pressing need for writing this book, I sought valuable advice from Bill Taverner and Jamye Waxman. Additionally, I have learned a great deal from each person interviewed for *Allies at Work*.

Some brief passages of earlier writing are included in this book. Amy Niedzalkoski, a talented attorney and educator, wrote some educational materials for a program we developed for high school Gay-Straight Alliances. Thank you to Amy for permitting modification of her facts of the case summary from *Lofton v. Kearney* for use in this book.

Excerpts from my dissertation on the history of marriage equality were an important inclusion. I want to thank my dissertation committee: Dr. Judy Alston, Dr. Jeanne Stanley, Dr. Brent Satterly, the Rev. Dr. Bill Stayton, and Dr. Don Dyson. Dr. Dyson, in his university courses, augments the Nelson continuum, discussed in this book, by adding a fifth stage, Advocacy. *Allies at Work* considers Advocacy as a subset of Full Acceptance, but is indebted to Dr. Dyson's vital work on the subject.

It is thanks to Out & Equal that this work has come to fruition. On a larger scale, it is difficult to imagine where workplace equality would be today if it were not for Out & Equal and their visionary, founding executive director, Selisse Berry. Selisse's editorial contributions were invaluable in improving *Allies at Work*. This book has provided me with an opportunity to work more intimately not just with Selisse, but also with the talented staff and organization that she has built.

There are many staff members at Out & Equal who deserve my thanks, including Pat Baillie, Stanley Ellicott, Stephen Gould, Kevin Shytle and Kevin Jones. Pat recognized the need for a strong training component and organized the first national speaking engagement for this book. Stanley led as coordinator and organized many of the myriad details to move this project forward. Stephen has been instrumental in developing grassroots interest and support across the country.

Most importantly, I thank Kevin Shytle and Kevin Jones. Kevin Shytle was Out & Equal's talented and dynamic managing director when this book was written. Kevin understood that *Allies at Work* was a necessary resource in the workplace and a vehicle for Out & Equal to have a significant impact there. Kevin's focus moved the project from manuscript to publication. Kevin Jones, Out & Equal's deputy director, managed the final process that ensured the book reached publication and made its way into the workplace.

In addition to their specific contributions, Out & Equal is also an organization that cares deeply about supporting my vision as an author. I have been treated as a valued partner. Their respect and spirit of collaboration speak volumes about the integrity of Out & Equal.

When I started writing, I reached out to two of my mentors, Dr. Richard Friend and Dr. Chris Bursk. Richard Friend, host of *Diversity Matters*, has been my mentor on corporate training since I entered the field. Richard provided a critical focus, clarity and pertinence to my writing.

Chris Bursk is the greatest teacher and humanitarian I have ever known. He was the first person who saw this book when it was a manuscript of only the first few chapters. In support of the project, he dedicated significant time and offered edits and insights that proved critical to the strength of this work.

I need to extend particular gratitude to Julia Hutton, the bright and hard-working editor of *Allies at Work*. More than just editing, she significantly contributed to the book's content and resources. She was able to help make this book more accessible and applicable for the workplace. Her efforts have been invaluable.

My children are too young to grasp what it means to write a book. However, I was aware of my work's impact when my three year-old daughter said that she would be late to a Labor Day picnic, because she had to stay home and write her book like Daddy. In no small part, this book is being written with the hope that they will grow into adults in a world in which they cannot even understand what the controversy regarding lesbian, gay, bisexual and transgender issues was all about.

My greatest ally is my best friend and spouse, Annie Hall. She has offered nothing but unwavering support during this process. With humor, candor and complete understanding, she has always offered not just support but enthusiasm for this work.

It is this combination of supporters, my allies, who helped with this book. I am deeply grateful, as their dedication and support have allowed it to reach publication.

The Importance of Allies

Selisse Berry
Founding Executive Director, Out & Equal Workplace Advocates

The work of Out & Equal is to create workplaces where we can bring all of who we are to work every day. Year after year the number of allies at the Out & Equal Workplace Summit grows significantly. I'm convinced we couldn't do this important work without these courageous colleagues and friends.

As the workplace becomes the main meeting ground for people from different backgrounds, the need for tolerance and cultural fluency continues to grow, enabling businesses and employees to flourish. *Allies at Work* brings new attention to a little-explored aspect of job site diversity: the ways that heterosexual coworkers can oppose discrimination and help create a fair work environment for lesbian, gay, bisexual and transgender (LGBT) employees.

The idea for this resource manual emerged a number of years ago as the impact of allies became clear. The book's development was spurred when diversity and human resources professionals expressed the need for materials on the topic so they could be more effective in their work. *Allies at Work* presents ideas for developing more open dialogue, examines common obstacles and reports success stories. It also shows that the most effective means of improving the workplace often comes down to human relationships—for which there's not exactly a blueprint! Being an ally involves getting to know your colleagues and building friendly, respectful work relationships with people who are different from you.

David M. Hall

Allies are essential to increasing equality in the workplace. They bring their sense of justice, personal support, talents, networks and numbers to assist their colleagues—and to create a workplace that better reflects their own values. Because they speak from a different vantage point, allies can get ideas and information across to people who might be resistant to an openly gay or transgender person. Allies may have more access to decision-makers and be able to speak up in management and board meetings where no LGBT person is present. Allies at every company level can be effective advocates for equal rights and can educate their peers and supervisors about LGBT diversity issues. And as many studies have shown, prejudice declines when people who are part of a majority group interact in an authentic way with people in a minority group. Allies' work relationships and accepting attitudes exert a positive influence on the broader environment.

For most of us, work is stressful enough without the added burdens of open or indirect hostility and prejudice—or the pressure to keep one's identity hidden for fear of reprisals. Lesbian, gay, bisexual and transgender employees face many expressions of discrimination on the job, and they need allies to help create and maintain a safe and fair work environment.

Institutional forms of discrimination include unequal health, family leave, bereavement and pension benefits. Other types of discrimination include inappropriate jokes, lectures about personal issues and religious beliefs, poor work reviews, transfers to less desirable worksites or being passed over for promotion. Being silenced or being given the silent treatment are other damaging forms of discrimination. Allies are needed as leaders and advocates of change for all these forms of discrimination, enabling LGBT employees to be more productive staff members, feel safer coming out and being out on the job, and be free to focus on just the same workday challenges as everybody else.

Allies get involved for many different reasons. Often it's just that they become better acquainted with an LGBT coworker and realize what an unfair situation that employee is dealing with. Many allies have insight into work equality issues because they have LGBT family members, friends or acquaintances. Some become allies because they attend work-related diversity trainings or seminars that give them new perspectives, sensitize them to the issues or correct misinformation. I've witnessed some striking moments at Out & Equal's annual Summits, when heterosexuals employees who attended—sometimes unwillingly—suddenly "got" the equality issues at stake and stood up to voice their new, sincere support for their LGBT colleagues.

I know firsthand what it's like to have career hopes and dreams dimmed by homophobia and discrimination. Though a divinity school graduate, I was unable to get ordained as an out lesbian and lead a church congregation. Years ago, when I looked at the choices before me, I decided that living my life openly and authentically was more important to me than anything else. But I also believe that no one should have to choose between a career they love and living life openly and with integrity. No one should have to cope with institutional or individual discrimination on the job. Out & Equal reflects my commitment to social justice and my enthusiasm for getting people talking, sharing resources and solving problems together.

In many religious and political circles, equality for lesbian, gay, bisexual and transgender Americans is still controversial. Over the last ten years, however, the private sector has made significant advances in employment equality. Today, 97% of the nation's largest companies include sexual orientation in their nondiscrimination policies, and 60% also include gender identity protections. More than half of Fortune 500 companies now offer their LGBT employees domestic partner benefits. Major employers are motivated to make these changes in order to retain staff and to gain a competitive edge in hiring from the broadest talent pool. They recognize that potential hires, straight or LGBT, size up an employer's benefits plan, and many valuable employees decide to stay at or leave a job based on its work climate and benefits package. Many savvy companies have found that LGBT equality is part of a productive workplace culture that's cohesive, accountable and good for the bottom line.

Changes at the corporate level are having a ripple effect through the whole business community and modeling good practices for smaller employers and other workplaces. But discrimination is still widespread and poses problems even within companies where top executives have put fair policies in place. Reaching out and letting coworkers know that you are an ally can make a difference. And whether you are an ally, lesbian, gay, bisexual or transgender, expanding your network and suggesting concrete ways to support diversity can contribute to a better atmosphere, one in which all employees can be comfortable being themselves.

I'd like to thank many people who shared their thoughts and talents during the development of this book. They include most especially author David M. Hall, whose passion for justice and education is the reason this book exists; the wonderful members of the Out & Equal team who were involved in the process of shepherding the book from inception to publication; our thoughtful and savvy editor Julia Hutton; and the many people who participated in *Allies at Work* interviews, including Tara Bunch, Chris Eagan, Heidi Green, Claire Lyons, Greg Nika, Brent Reinhard, Marcelo Roman, Marla Schlenoff, Amanda Simpson, Janet Smith, Mike Syers, Neal Walton, Adam Wolf and Louise Young.

And a special thank you to all our allies who have the courage and commitment to stand up for equality and justice. Thank you for making a difference and changing the world, one cubicle at a time.

Becoming an Ally

My personal journey has resulted in my developing a great sense of responsibility for being an ally. I am an ally today because I was taught the value and necessity of working for equality for those who are lesbian, gay, bisexual and transgender. It is my responsibility not only to be an ally but also to help others understand how to be effective allies. There is an especially critical need to address this topic where people earn their livelihood. A productive workplace needs allies, not adversaries. Organizational effectiveness is significantly enhanced when we replace adversarial situations with ones founded on alliances and mutual respect. Respecting differences is important, but it is even more useful and rewarding to respect common interests. This book examines and models ways to implement a diversity program that addresses the workplace challenges facing lesbian, gay, bisexual and transgender workers and their colleagues and employers.

We need not only to promote increased discourse and training on the issues facing lesbian, gay, bisexual and transgender individuals in the workplace, but also to encourage the development of allies in the workplace. By "allies," I mean heterosexuals who are open, appreciative and even advocates for people who have a different sexual orientation or gender identity/expression.

The goal of workplace discourse and training on issues facing those who are lesbian, gay, bisexual and transgender is not simply to make everyone "nicer" but to improve productivity. Conflict undermines the teamwork necessary for success in a business. Providing a structure for better analysis, communication and teamwork can help end discrimination—intentional and unintentional—and change corporate culture.

My own history and work as a diversity trainer have shown me that, with education and support, the workplace can be a productive place, no matter what one's sexual orientation or gender identity/expression. However, a productive work environment will rarely, if ever, develop on its own. Instead, it takes hard work, a willingness to grow and a commitment to changing the existing culture of the workplace.

My advocacy arises from the simplest of origins. I was raised to be a caring person, and my outlook broadened to include those who are lesbian, gay, bisexual and transgender when I was a junior in high school. It was 1989, and it was the first time someone told me that lesbian, gay, bisexual and transgender individuals were no different than anyone else. That was the start of an evolving journey that ultimately led to writing this book.

Evolving is an important word choice, as I have learned that passion and hard work are not enough for lesbian, gay, bisexual and transgender advocacy. Later in this book, I'll examine the ongoing personal growth and reflection that heterosexual privilege requires—and how what goes unexamined or taken for granted can limit an ally's voice. Regular self-analysis is necessary to ensure that lesbian, gay, bisexual and transgender voices and narratives are not just respected but understood. Having unearned privilege can make truly understanding oppression difficult. This can lead to unintended consequences, including unwittingly marginalizing the voices that allies intend to champion.

Many of us learn as young children about heterosexual privilege. No one ever names it or specifically mentions it to us. In a way, something more damaging occurs. All too often, heterosexual privilege is interwoven into the fabric of our childhood and escapes examination and reflection.

As a ten year-old boy, I was riding bikes with my neighbor after school one spring afternoon when he yelled to me, "Do you know what gay stands for?"

"What?" I played along.

"Got AIDS yet?"

We both laughed, certain that AIDS, or even homosexuality for that matter, would never enter our world.

I was born in 1974. While growing up, not a single one of my peers was openly gay. In fact, no one I was acquainted with or even knew of was openly gay. As far as I knew, there were no gay relatives, friends, teachers, doctors or neighbors. Gay was just something I had heard mentioned—and then only as a disparaging and belittling term. My friends and I heard homophobic jokes and repeated them with little thought. We would tease each other with accusations of being gay. We did so before we even knew what homosexuality was.

Our intolerance was entirely directed at gay men. As a child, I don't think I even thought about lesbians or bisexuals. Hearing the word "transgender" would have prompted a blank look, as if I were listening to another language.

The homophobia and heterosexism that I grew up with came not so much from explicit messages but from implicit ones. I never seriously considered whether homosexuality was right or wrong. I don't recall anybody ever telling me that homosexuality was immoral or a psychiatric disorder. I just came to believe that there had to be something wrong with gay people. It is essential to my story to note that I learned this not just through homophobic jokes but also through heterosexist silence.

A child receives a powerful message when the only time that an identity is referred to is when it is being belittled and mocked. However, the silence I encountered was even more powerful. I was never told that being gay was normal. I never heard an adult correct a joke about homosexuality. Surely some adult would have

Important Concept what else Do we keep quiet about?

done so, if our taunts and jests were wrong, and someone would have made sure to explain that homosexuality was okay. While I was never told that homosexuality was wrong, I was also never told that homosexuality was accepted. The pervasive silence served as a *de facto* endorsement of homophobia and heterosexism.

Not until much later would I come to learn that there were gay people in my world. Since I was heterosexual and assumed that everyone else was as well, I had little reason to think about the pain of homophobia and heterosexism. The nature of privilege, in this case heterosexual privilege, is that people aren't aware of their own privilege unless someone opens their eyes to it and challenges their assumptions. What makes the universal assumption of heterosexuality even more painful for those who are lesbian, gay or bisexual is that if everyone is assumed to be heterosexual, then heterosexuality defines what is normal. Consequently, people who are lesbian, gay or bisexual come to be regarded as abnormal and even subversive. Transgender individuals often encounter even greater bias.

Today I am an adult ally who works passionately for lesbian, gay, bisexual and transgender social justice. What motivated this change in outlook since my childhood?

I grew up in a loving household. My mother taught me to see the best in people. I was expected to be caring and kind, and I was held to that standard. No one taught me to exclude gay people from that compassionate outlook on the world, but I was never taught to include them, either.

In my 11th grade human sexuality class, we discussed homosexuality in an informational, deliberative context for the first time in my life. There were no gay jokes allowed. My classroom instructor, Steve Harnish, was the type of teacher who connects with his students through his honesty and sincerity. Through education, he challenged the messages that I had received throughout my life.

He explained to us that homosexuality is just as acceptable as heterosexuality. He taught us that in 1975 the American Psychiatric

Association had definitively stated that homosexuality was not a psychiatric disorder.* What he taught us was certainly challenged by students in class. Some insisted that homosexuality had to be a psychiatric disorder.

For me, acceptance came quickly, perhaps because I had never been told by the important people in my world—such as parents, teachers and clergy—that homosexuality was morally wrong. For those who have been taught that homosexuality is morally wrong, it may be that they face a longer path or a less certain journey toward acceptance. This is a reality we must contend with in any program, whether in a workplace or a school.

My teacher quickly changed my biased beliefs and assumptions. I realized that I had been wrong, and my recently held views, which I now despised, weighed heavily on my conscience. In fact, my reaction provided a foundation for the start of my political awakening.

I wish that this awakening had come earlier. The previous summer, two of my new friends had bragged about how, a year before, they had vandalized a gay man's house, "a faggot's house," they explained, until he moved out of the neighborhood. One friend particularly liked to boast about it in front of his father. I let my friends know that I believed what they did was wrong. Looking back on the situation, I think I should have voiced far more outrage. I did not express my true indignation to them until my high school teacher, Mr. Harnish, educated me with factual information and normalized homosexuality. This was one of my first lessons in life about the power and subsequent pain of silence.

•The American Psychiatric Association's reclassification of homosexuality as normal followed years of demonstrations and pressure from gay activists—along with 25 years of increased scientific research on homosexuality. Gay activists (and some APA members) were influenced by the 1960s civil rights and feminist movements, which had catalyzed broad support for social equality. The APA removed homosexuality from its list of psychiatric disorders in 1973. Fact-based medical research continues to confirm the decision, though some controversy—and a conservative minority—still exists within the APA. In 1991, the World Health Organization also removed homosexuality as an illness from their classification of diseases.

This is an unusual brand of guilt. I did not participate in the vandalism, and my peers who carried out the harassment were not even my friends when the vandalism occurred. I had never met their gay neighbor, yet I felt as though I knew the man who had been tormented. Reflecting on the incident now, I see the faces of my many gay friends whom I love so dearly. How could there have been a time that I was just a passive bystander? The painful conclusion that I have reached is that until the 11th grade, I was part of the epidemic of silence. Though I never threw a rock at the gay man's house myself, those rocks were hurled as a result of a collective silence in which I took part. Today I realize that all who are silent share responsibility for the pain and discrimination inflicted on those who are lesbian, gay, bisexual and transgender. In the workplace, the legacy of long-standing bias and silence can negatively affect organizational development and productivity.

Through education, I found my voice. In many ways, this book is a call to action for more education. Although I would not have been able to name them succinctly at the time, I first recognized privilege, bias and oppression in contemporary American society when I was in 11th grade. In my social studies classes, I had learned about inequality throughout history and across cultures, but my junior year was the first time that I was challenged to see injustice in my own world. I was pained by my discovery of discrimination, and I felt driven to work for equity. However, I had few ideas as to what concrete steps I could take. In that era, there was certainly no Gay-Straight Alliance on my high school campus.

In 12th grade, I took our school's elective human sexuality course. Our teacher, Dr. Konnie McCaffree, was a nationally renowned sexologist. She challenged us with affective, cognitive and behavioral activities to better understand the pain and isolation of being lesbian, gay, bisexual or transgender in our society. Her lessons, along with the curriculum she wrote, transformed my worldview.

Dr. McCaffree faced some resistance from her pupils. I recall two or three students using the word "faggot" in class, and she would challenge and educate them, communicating with passion and patience. In addition to classroom instruction, she loaned me Brian McNaught's book *On Being Gay.* Up to that point, I had no idea that books had been written on the topic of homosexuality. His book painfully illustrated the impact of anti-gay discrimination and bigotry. Reading it, I was outraged by the bias and hatred that existed. I could hardly fathom how anti-gay attitudes permeated our society and could no longer relate to the person I had been just a year earlier, who had not been attuned to any of this injustice.

As part of the educational unit on sexual orientation, Dr. Mc-Caffree invited a graduate of our school, a man named Scott, who was openly gay and in his twenties, as a guest speaker for our class. I was already fully accepting of homosexuality, but I was surprised to learn that someone who had graduated from my own school was actually gay. Certainly no one had come out while we were in high school. I was excited that for the first time in my life, I was going to meet someone who was openly gay.

When I walked into class, I could not believe what I saw. I had grown up with stereotypes and had learned that gay men were weak and effeminate, yet there before us stood perhaps the strongest and most muscular man I had ever met in my life. While in school, Scott had not been in theater but in sports; he was a wrestler. When I heard him speak, he did not articulate his words with the stereotypical gay lisp. In just a few minutes, I had clear evidence that everything I had learned about homosexuality was at best a fabrication and at worst a form of oppression, forcing an identity into a box and denying individuals power and status in the larger culture.

I realized that I had been lied to prior to attending these classes. The lie, however, did not consist of spoken words. Instead, it was a lie in the perception and treatment of an entire group of people.

When I met Scott and read McNaught's book, I already knew that the American Psychological Association had concluded that homosexuality was normal. What I had not fully realized until walking into my classroom the day that Scott spoke to us was that the social construction of "the homosexual" was a work of fiction. This construction, which is damaging to lesbian, gay, bisexual and transgender people, provides further power and privilege to those who are heterosexual. That realization marked a turning point, and it fueled my drive and sense of responsibility to work to fight inequity and the unearned privilege that I now recognized and also understood came at other people's expense.

I began volunteering for sexuality-related agencies and was contemplating a career in human sexuality education. Shortly after high school graduation, I testified before the Senate Education Committee in favor of including sexual orientation and gender identity in the Outcomes Based Education diversity standards. I volunteered as an AIDS buddy and community health educator. I became an officer in my college's Open Door Club, a predecessor to Gay-Straight Alliances. Dr. Konnie McCaffree had opened up many of those doors for me.

My political awakening would grow and expand far beyond lesbian, gay, bisexual and transgender issues; I even ran for state legislator when I was 26 years old. However, I ultimately came back to where my political awakening began: earning my doctorate, writing a dissertation on the politics of same-sex marriage, advising a Gay-Straight Alliance, teaching a graduate course on lesbian, gay, bisexual and transgender issues, co-founding Out & Equal Greater Philadelphia, and providing training across the country on lesbian, gay, bisexual and transgender diversity and cultural competency.

Today we live in a decidedly different world for lesbian, gay, bisexual and transgender individuals than the one in which I grew up. In many workplaces, there are company-supported groups working to eventually eliminate discrimination and bias based on sexual orientation or gender identity, as evidenced by the growing number of lesbian, gay, bisexual and transgender Employee Resource Groups, internal corporate-sponsored groups for networking around a common interest. High school and college students often join Gay-Straight Alliances, the school equivalent of an Employee Resource Group, and many of these students are unwilling to re-enter the closet when they become corporate employees. Those who choose to reenter the closet will find their own unique set of challenges, including difficulty giving their full energy to their careers and the best interests of the company. In many segments of society, it is far more common today to know someone who is openly gay than it has ever been before. The percentage of openly lesbian, gay, bisexual and transgender individuals in the workplace is growing.

Yet homophobia and heterosexism still persist, and the implications are not just painful but sometimes tragic. In 2008, Lawrence King, an 8th grader in California, was shot and killed at school by one of his classmates for being gay.[1] Steve Stanton, for 14 years the city manager of Largo, Florida, was fired for undergoing hormone therapy and planning to have sex-reassignment surgery.[2] In the United States military, it is still policy to fire someone for being openly lesbian or gay.[3] At the time of this writing, there is no federal protection in the workplace against discrimination due to sexual orientation or gender identity. Many individuals have worked for years to pass the Employment Non-Discrimination Act, which would bar workplace discrimination. While its chance of passage has increased, the final version of the bill is at issue. It is still unclear whether the bill will include both sexual orientation and identity or only sexual orientation.[4] Despite the remarkable progress made since my own days as a teenager, true equality remains far from being realized. In fact, Americans face towering barriers to fully transforming the

David M. Hall

ways in which people who are lesbian, gay, bisexual or transgender are treated and valued.

Allies have a responsibility and a unique role in working to ensure a more just and equitable society for our lesbian, gay, bisexual and transgender family members, friends and coworkers. I discovered my passion for justice in high school, and this led me to become an ally. Today, through sometimes trying and emotional experiences of advocacy, I better understand the powerful role that allies play. One recent community-based experience provides a sad and powerful example.

A school district in New Jersey included in their third-grade curriculum the video *That's a Family*, a documentary about non-traditional families that included gay and lesbian parents. Some parents in the district were angry that the video was being shown, and they began to organize a community-wide protest. This protest captured the attention of the national media.

The school district organized a community meeting to show the documentary and allow discussion about how the film met the state mandate for family life education. The room was packed with hundreds of people, many of whom were infuriated that children were learning that some families have same-sex parents. Some in the crowd were screaming at school officials: "What gives you the right? I teach tolerance at home!"

If some of your lesbian, gay, bisexual or transgender co-workers had attended this meeting, how do you think that they would have felt? How productive do you think that they would have been at work the next day? How would the experience have impacted them, if they were in the closet? What does such an event demonstrate about the challenges faced by lesbian, gay, bisexual and transgender individuals? What support could a strong allies program offer when someone is feeling attacked, vulnerable or angry?

Those at the meeting who supported the school's curriculum, particularly those who were gay and lesbian, understood that many

Good to know [margin annotation]

people in the crowd were enraged. It took great courage for lesbian and gay residents to speak in front of this infuriated crowd. Some found such courage. Many others understandably chose silence.

I attended this community meeting with a colleague. He is a college professor who speaks at international conferences and sits on the boards of national organizations. He receives exemplary evaluations from his students. A young leader in his field, he is also gay.

To properly understand this story, the reader needs to understand that I do not have any of the physical characteristics that are stereotypically associated with gay men. People never assume that I am gay by looking at me. In contrast, my colleague finds that people sometimes assume that he is gay.

He and I both lined up behind the microphone to share our comments in support of the curriculum. He stood a few people ahead of me. When he reached the microphone, a number of people in the crowd yelled at him: "There's the guy with the homosexual agenda!" Another screamed, "Where do your kids go to school?" while contemptuous laughter erupted. And then another person shouted, "Where do you pay your taxes?" My colleague completed his articulate, well-considered comments. Few people were listening.

Twenty minutes later, I had the opportunity to speak. I had carefully formulated my thoughts. When I reached the microphone, I spoke uninterrupted.

Later that night, we laughed about how crazy, ignorant and stupid some of the people in attendance had been. Back at his home, we performed for his husband and gave our best impressions of the meeting's bigots. I soon realized, however, that our laughter was really a way of protecting ourselves from what was a painful evening. That protection would prove to be short-lived.

My colleague and I belong to a national Listserv with a number of people who were at the school district's community meeting that evening. Over the following days, we were corresponding about this meeting over the Listserv. Keep in mind that the only supposed controversy was the documentary film's depiction of gay and lesbian parents among the array of happy, well-adjusted families. There was probably no one on the Listserv who considered this content controversial. Everyone on the email list who lived in the area was urged to attend the upcoming school board meeting about this video.

In response, my colleague who was heckled and belittled wrote to our Listserv, "I am glad that I was there to lend my support. But I am not going to attend the next meeting. I think that this is a forum for straight allies. There was no room for my voice."

I read this brief email, and my eyes welled up. How could someone so bright and so accomplished have his voice effectively shut down? There was room for my voice, but only because of oppression, bias and privilege. I found myself crying, eventually sobbing, simultaneously furious, saddened and wounded.

I continually struggle to grasp the magnitude of hatred that exists, though I seek to comprehend it. It is at times like this that I remind myself of *Cat's Cradle,* the great book by Kurt Vonnegut. A plague strikes an island, and people keep dying. A young boy wakes one night and sits with his father, a surgeon, while he is operating on a dying patient. The person dies, and the doctor begins laughing hysterically. Still laughing, he takes his son by the hand and grabs a flashlight. He walks his son outside to where dead bodies are piled up as a consequence of the plague. He shines his flashlight across the piles of dead bodies.

Like any parent who wants to leave some sort of inheritance to a child, he says, "Son, one day this will all be yours."

Vonnegut's dark humor and powerful insight remind us that we inherit the real world, which has suffering and pain as well as happiness and joy. While there are limits to what we can do to change the world, many of us still try. In so doing, we are sometimes, perhaps even often, able to create meaningful change within our world. Some people even manage to leave a legacy that has forever altered human society.

It is critical to help allies better understand and utilize the power of their voices. Allies' voices can create a more just work and community environment. Allies supporting their lesbian, gay, bisexual and transgender colleagues can play an important and even essential role in changing corporate culture.

The intervention of my 11th and 12th grade teachers was the catalyst for profound personal change of such magnitude that lesbian, gay, bisexual and transgender advocacy has become one of my life's greatest passions. Many of our colleagues at work are ready to support our efforts and even to lead them. Often, they have not had the kind of classroom intervention that I had experienced. Or perhaps in the past, they weren't ready for such a transformational moment. However, they may well be open and willing to learn. That can turn into a passion to lead. It is in our best interest to teach and inspire them, to provide an intervention that disrupts the homophobic and heterosexist threads that are woven into the fabric of our society.

Throughout this book, there are case studies to explain various concepts, theories and statistics, to illustrate the main points under discussion. These case studies serve as reminders that we are dealing not just with issues, but also with human beings. The impact of workplace inequity is not just theoretical but, for too many, personally painful. The pain interferes with effective organizational development.

This is a cause that requires courage, passion, tenacity and patience. Equity for lesbian, gay, bisexual and transgender people is often referred to in the national media as part of a culture war. While it is not a literal war, the use of a violent metaphor reflects the reality that people truly get hurt and become proverbial casualties in this struggle. In many instances, lesbian, gay, bisexual and transgender individuals stand up, sometimes at great personal risk, because they can no longer remain silent. Allies have a responsibility to stand with them. Corporations that support their workers find that doing so is in their economic best interest. This book examines how we develop that awareness and effectively build ally support and advocacy.

It is the intent of this work to serve as a practical guide to workplace inclusion. Throughout, you will find citations of valuable theories and frameworks. In each and every case, theories are provided with pertinent workplace examples. In the spirit of the great John Dewey, theory will never be utilized apart from doing. This work is designed to give busy professionals a high quality resource that is easily accessible and applicable for their workplace.

In an effort to enhance organizational development and effectiveness, this book aims to foster a more inclusive work environment. The content is especially relevant to the U.S. workforce in terms of the history and law that is cited. While *Allies at Work* has implications that are transferable across cultures, the steps to counter discrimination and increase workplace productivity will be decidedly different in countries where homosexuality is widely accepted than in those where homosexuality is illegal.

Most chapters contain a *Tips for Success* box. This can be used to reference key issues addressed in each chapter and to highlight particular aspects of the broad discussion about workplace diversity and inclusion. *Tips for Success* does not outline each chapter, but instead focuses on key issues necessary to understand the topic.

This book provides a strong grounding in history and theoretical issues, to equip the reader to analyze and articulate the reasons and ways that his or her company should change in order to maximize capacity and ensure a highly productive work environment. The text includes an examination of the long, painful history of persecution of lesbian, gay, bisexual and transgender people. This aspect of American history is often left out of our textbooks in high school and college. However, a basic understanding of institutionalized bias and discrimination in the U.S. is necessary to fully prepare for the challenges ahead in expanding diversity and inclusion in each corporation. The legacy of bias and persecution still impacts our society.

Allies at Work also gives you research-based strategies for creating change in policy and law. It is this very process that moves us from discussion to action. Conversation and commentary may be given high priority within an organization, but they are not enough to bring about the necessary changes that foster equity and more effective organizational development.

A Note about Allies

What this book offers is a way to change the dynamics of a workplace around issues of sexual orientation and gender identity/expression. The change is primarily a linguistic one with practical applications. I use the word "allies" in this book to refer to those within the heterosexual population who constitute a community of support for people of a different sexual orientation, identity or expression. The term "allies" describes the experience of a growing number of Americans who are participating in the evolution that is occurring in our society. As more and more people begin to understand and accept those with a different sexual orientation or gender identity/expression, we have an opportunity to create a support network for people, including coworkers, who still face widespread discrimination and prejudice. For heterosexual allies, this book speaks to a responsibility to develop greater workplace equity.

The very language that we use to reflect the reality we encounter can also serve to shape that reality.

The author understands that there are also applications of "ally" within the lesbian, gay, bisexual and transgender population. This text addresses the universal issues of being an ally which apply to everyone, including those who are lesbian, gay, bisexual, or transgender.

David M. Hall

Allies at Work is a tool for all allies to develop the necessary cultural competency within a corporation to foster maximum workplace productivity. These pages focus on what unites allies, rather than what divides them.

CHAPTER ONE

Language about Homosexuality

People are not born allies. Hatred and discrimination are learned, and it is unlikely that someone can grow up in American society without hearing negative and even hateful things being said about lesbian, gay, bisexual and transgender individuals. However, as history and especially civil rights advances show, hatred and discrimination can also be unlearned. This book is meant to serve as a catalyst for waking up allies for action.

The Power of Language

In order to understand the possibilities inherent in changing corporate culture regarding sexual orientation and gender identity/ expression, we first need to examine the language we use to discuss these issues and then the surrounding social context. While language, particularly about diversity and identity, is fluid and subject to change, we risk making allies afraid to advocate for our cause if they believe that they cannot use basic phrases and categories without offending. This anxiety is exacerbated by the fact that we lack consensus about the most inclusive and effective way to define and categorize people who are lesbian, gay, bisexual and transgender. The varied and evolving terminology is problematic and often inhibits the very changes that we champion. The challenge of language and the feelings surrounding it merit careful examination.

In this chapter, I address how to navigate issues around language and lesbian, gay, bisexual and transgender issues. This chapter is not meant to create a conclusive approach to language. Instead, it examines the rationale for my own language choices. In addition, it provides examples for negotiating the fluid and sensitive terrain of communication. See Figure 1.1 for *Tips for Success* in your own workplace. This chapter is meant to facilitate the understanding of language choices in diversity work. Rather than calling for universal adoption of my own conclusions, this is a starting point for talking about sensitive issues in your workplace.

FIGURE 1.1

Tips for Success: Allies and Language

1. **Diversity and inclusion language is fluid.** The norms and rules will change, so it is valuable to have ongoing communication.
2. **Do not let one person speak for an entire group.** Understand that individual uses of language will vary within the same group. For example, many gay men may refer to themselves as *gay* while some will refer to themselves as *queer*.
3. **Communicate about communication.** Ask people what they prefer. Share with them what you know about the topic.
4. **Stress to others the power of language.** Some of our colleagues may not understand the power and impact of using language that others find hurtful or disempowering. Conversely, they may not understand the power and impact of language that others find respectful and empowering.

A few years ago, I was invited to give a presentation on being out in the workplace at a Conference Board diversity conference.

At the opening reception, I talked with a human resources diversity executive, and she expressed excitement about my upcoming session. It was important to her, she said, that her company do more to create an equitable environment for gay employees. She had been advocating for change, though she had met with some resistance.

The next day, I started my presentation with the subject of language. I offered a long but abbreviated version of the alphabet soup abbreviation: LGBTQQA, which stands for lesbian, gay, bisexual, transgender, queer, questioning and allies. I explained what each letter stood for and what each word meant, and I began to address some of the unique challenges that would be experienced in the workplace for each of these orientations and identities.

The woman I had spoken with at the reception raised her hand. Based on our earlier conversation, I expected her to be an active and supportive workshop participant, and I was eager to provide whatever clarification and support I could. However, she raised her hand not to further absorb what I was saying but to challenge it.

"Why do the letters keep changing?" she asked, clearly frustrated. "When I last went over this with my colleagues, it was GLBT. Now the L comes first, and there are additional letters. It is already very difficult for me to get people at my workplace on board with this issue. If the language keeps changing, it is going to be even more difficult."

I explained that a significant challenge of this work is that language on the topic is fluid. We discussed the importance of creating a basic language within the workplace, while also respecting differences that exist within the lesbian, gay, bisexual and transgender community. There is a lack of consensus about language, so I introduce my audience to the diversity of perspectives that exist, but I also encourage employers to be aware of the variety in language or acronyms they choose to use in the workplace. This led to a valuable discussion about the larger issue of fluid language among a wide variety of minority groups.

David M. Hall

As I left the conference, I reflected on the implications of her message. I realized that many of my trainings are in professional circles in academic and nonprofit settings. Among these professionals, concerns about feelings are sometimes paramount. As a result, considerable thought is given to reexamining and refining language, and so acronyms and identity terms continue to change and evolve. I came to realize that hypersensitivity and hyper-specificity were proving to be considerable obstacles in communicating with people outside of this arena. Indeed, with an issue so important, we can scarcely afford such a disconnect.

If we are just talking to each other, to our colleagues in the field of diversity training on lesbian, gay, bisexual and transgender issues, then fluid terminology rarely causes problems. In fact, it is even beneficial, because it allows marginalized individuals and groups ample room to define themselves. However, when we move beyond this circle, language that is highly specialized becomes elitist and exclusionary.

The woman in my session was dedicating seventy-five minutes to the topic of equity in the workplace for those who are lesbian, gay, bisexual and transgender. That may have been the only training that she received all year or longer on the subject matter. She resented the time that was invested in reframing language, because for her this was a secondary concern. My desire to maximize the inclusiveness of my message actually ran counter to her efforts to maximize the inclusiveness of her workplace.

The question of language is by no means a new one. In 1951, Donald Webster Cory wrote *The Homosexual in America*. He noted the following: "Needed for years was an ordinary, everyday, matter-of-fact word that could express the concept of homosexuality without glorification or condemnation."[5] Over a half-century later, we are sometimes dedicating significant energy to the very same problem. Sometimes it seems that our hours dedicated to developing inclusive language result not in resolution, but in continuing to devote time to discussing inclusive language.

Alphabet Soup

Let's start by exploring the terminology that best describes people whose livelihoods are at stake in what has almost always been a heterosexual province: corporate and business culture. A common solution for communication is the alphabet soup abbreviation, which allows a quick, concise way to include a wide variety of orientations and identities. For example, G commonly stands for the word "gay" and L for "lesbian." However, there are a few challenges with the alphabet soup acronym or abbreviation. A significant one, just to start with, is the quantity and "proper" order of the letters. Some companies and organizations use LGBT, while others use GLBT. And others use LGBTQ, with the Q signifying either "queer" or "questioning." In academia, I have actually seen some use of LG-BTTSIQQAA. This substantial block of letters stands for "lesbian, gay, bisexual, transgender, two-spirit, intersex, queer, questioning, asexual and allies." The Intersex Society of North America defines intersex as "a general term used for a variety of conditions in which a person is born with a reproductive or sexual anatomy that doesn't seem to fit the typical definitions of female or male."[6] It typically refers to genetic variations, such as XXY chromosomes, and to anatomical variations. While LGBTTSIQQAA maximizes inclusiveness, its length defeats the very purpose of an abbreviation.

It's likely that whatever terms appear in this or any book will become antiquated over time, because language is constantly changing. Educator and writer Brian McNaught argues that acronyms and abbreviations should be avoided, because they keep people from saying actual words, such as "transgender." McNaught contends that we would never reduce racial minorities to a list of acronyms.

He argues that acronyms, if used at all, should be used as little as possible. He wants people to say "lesbian," "gay," "bisexual" and "transgender" as much as possible.[7]

McNaught explains that the acronym is also ineffective, because it can interfere with clear communication. "It is confusing to people who don't know what the term means. As educators, why should we leave everyone behind by using a word that they don't understand?"[8]

Another consideration for communication is the use of the word "queer." Some colleges have Queer Studies departments. One benefit of the term "queer" is that, in contrast to the word "gay," it is neither gendered nor anchored in sexual orientation, and so is more inclusive of people who are transgender. For example, Eli Green, founder and chair of the Association for Gender Research, Education, Action and Academics (AGREAA) identifies as gender queer. He explains, "I identify as gender queer—as non-transitioning transgender.... I would say that the reason I use the word queer for my identity is that there is no other term. When I use queer, I mean it as not heterosexual."[9] For Green, queer is the most inclusive language that he feels fits his identity. However, a significant limitation to this term is that "queer" has historically been used for humiliation and oppression. So, understandably, many people find the use of the word in any context hurtful and demeaning.

There exists a wide range of additional options. For this book, I have decided to write out the words lesbian, gay, bisexual and transgender—or a shortened list only when referring to a specific subset of this group. Set out repeatedly on the page, the phrase is longer than any author would like. However, after a long process of weighing other approaches, I find this the best way to navigate the sensitive field of diversity inclusion. Off the page and out in the real world, I find that in conversation, it is much easier to name all the different identities and move away from using abbreviations.

Homophobia and Heterosexism: Some Definitions and Examples

As we consider what language best reflects our diversity, we must also closely examine the bias faced by lesbian, gay, bisexual and transgender individuals, as well as the subsequent language employed in describing discriminatory treatment. Let's consider, for example, the words "homophobia" and "heterosexism."

Congressman Joseph Sestak, a Democratic congressman from Pennsylvania, won his seat in 2006 in a predominantly Republican district in suburban Philadelphia. A former vice admiral in the Navy, Sestak opposes the long-standing military policy of expelling people from the military for being lesbian, gay, bisexual or transgender. Explains Sestak: "I can remember when outstanding servicemen with all the qualifications you could ask for approached me to start to tell me that they were gay, and all that went through my mind was, 'Please don't tell me. You're too talented. We can't afford to lose you.'"[10]

In some cases, the result of discrimination is not being terminated from your job, but being reminded by your colleagues that they do not consider your orientation to be equal or even worthy of respect. Jacqueline Thomas recalls the messages that she faced when working for a law firm: "I am a 42-year-old black, gay woman.... I started a temporary job in the accounting department of a law firm. In the beginning, the atmosphere there seemed workable. But within a week, someone decided I was gay, and, soon after, the offensive comments started. One day, the uncle of the woman I worked for came into the office and asked me on a date, saying, 'If you go out with me, you won't be gay anymore.' A couple of days later, a co-worker asked me if I wanted to have a smoke with her. I said OK. She later said that AIDS existed because of people like me."[11]

David M. Hall

Prejudiced work environments, like those described above, make it difficult, if not impossible, for lesbian, gay, bisexual and transgender individuals to fully perform their jobs to their best potential. It is also important to carefully define the language that we use to describe incidents and environments of discrimination. While such incidents are often described as examples of *homophobia*, they are actually examples of *heterosexism*.

A phobia is an irrational fear. When you have a phobia, you either flee what you fear or attack and attempt to destroy what you fear. Matthew Shepard and Lawrence King were victims of homophobia. Shepard was a twenty-one-year-old college student, murdered in an anti-gay hate crime near Laramie, Wyoming in 1998. Lawrence King was an openly gay fifteen-year-old, fatally shot in 2008 at his junior high school by a classmate. Across the country, people who are fired from their jobs for being lesbian, gay, bisexual, or transgender are victims of homophobia.

There are significant differences between homophobia and other phobias. For example, if you had ophidiophobia, a fear of snakes, you would probably recognize that your fear is irrational. However, people who exhibit homophobia often assume that they are normal and believe that those who consider homosexuality normal are the ones with an irrational world view. An additional concern about the term "homophobia" is that calling prejudice a phobia strikes some as an excuse for behaviors that can be dangerous and even fatal. Unlike people with other kinds of phobias, those who hate and fear homosexuals have often been taught to hate.

When people speak about homophobia, they are often speaking of heterosexism. I define heterosexism as the belief that heterosexuality is superior to homosexuality and deserves certain rights and privileges enshrined into law and custom.

Heterosexism is in evidence when companies fire lesbian, gay, bisexual and transgender individuals. Heterosexism is visible when parents disown their lesbian, gay, bisexual or transgender children. It underlies the belief that same-sex parents should be denied the right to adopt children. It treats lesbian, gay, bisexual and transgender relationships as undeserving of equality.

Heterosexism and homophobia in this book are also used to include discrimination based on gender identity/expression. Examples include discrimination for "cross-dressing" and denial of health insurance benefits for hormone therapy. People who are discriminated against because of their gender identity/expression often experience more extreme discrimination than those who experience prejudice due to sexual orientation. In fact, much of the heterosexist animosity directed toward gays and lesbians is based on projection of atypical gender mannerisms.

Feel free to reject the specific terms or language framework made in this text. What is important is to create a common language to use in your workplace. The primary goal should be finding language that is both inclusive and accessible. This chapter explains the terminology explored in this book, but the vocabulary used in the discussion here presents only a starting point for the larger society.

Allies have a critical role to play in the struggle for lesbian, gay, bisexual and transgender equality in the workplace. I believe that those with privilege have a responsibility to counter and even confront the epidemic of silence and discrimination that normalizes heterosexuality at the expense of lesbian, gay, bisexual and transgender individuals.

This book casts new light on heterosexual privilege and helps people recognize that the larger workplace culture benefits, if an environment of equity is valued and fostered. Lesbian, gay, bisexual and transgender employees and their allies are calling for changes in the work arena and culture, and *Allies at Work* provides part of the foundation for building lasting change within the corporate culture.

CHAPTER TWO

Allies & Adversaries: Real Opposition & Real Steps to Support Diversity

"...God Hates Fags and God Hates America."
www.godhatesfags.com

"It is the avenue chosen by homosexuals to gain access into jobs for the sole purpose of recruiting children into an extremely dangerous and unhealthy lifestyles [sic]. Because the majority of Americans oppose their tactics, they need the government's endorsement and muscle to get to our kids."

> **Don Wildmon,**
> **President of the American Family Association,**
> **comment on the Employment Non-Discrimination Act**

Allies need to understand the severe legal and social challenges facing lesbian, gay, bisexual and transgender individuals. We need to recognize the outright hostility directed toward them as well as the subtler heterosexism they face. What I propose is not just the promotion of diversity training, though that is essential, but also encouragement of allies in the workplace, people who are appreciative and supportive of their lesbian, gay, bisexual and transgender colleagues. Allies can help their colleagues who are coping with negative, misleading public perceptions of lesbian, gay, bisexual and transgender individuals—views put forward by a small, vociferous core of homophobic antagonists. Allies can advocate for diversity training that addresses sexual orientation and gender identity. Allies can also help their lesbian, gay, bisexual and transgender colleagues who are dealing with insensitive corporate environments and a flawed and discriminatory body of family law.

FIGURE 2.1

Tips for Success: Controversy and
Workplace Productivity

1. **Divisive social issues should have no impact on the workplace.** While lesbian, gay, bisexual and transgender issues are often a divisive issue in American political life, the corporation working to improve organizational development cannot afford to contribute to the oppression of some of its workers.

2. **It is about equal rights.** Lesbian, gay, bisexual and transgender workers face real discrimination and lack adequate legal protection. It is in the best interest of the corporation to provide equal protection regardless of sexual orientation and gender identity.

3. **It is an ongoing process.** Creating an equitable work environment requires extensive and ongoing work. Changing the corporate culture is difficult, but it is a wise investment.

4. **Anti-gay bias and hostility outside of work add considerable stress.** Lesbian, gay, bisexual and transgender families cope with specific stresses. Outside the company setting, they may regularly encounter bias and resistance that is never experienced by their heterosexual colleagues.

This chapter's overview of the workplace climate and subsequent challenges addresses three major areas: public perception, corporate policies and family law. These topics are explored here to deepen understanding of the ways that heterosexism impacts individuals in the workplace. In fact, public perception and family law can have a direct and significant impact on a person's workplace disposition and efficiency.

Federal and State Law, ENDA and Public Debate

Employment Non-Discrimination Act (ENDA) would make it illegal to fire someone due to sexual orientation, gender identity or expression.[12] Many people are under the mistaken impression that such discrimination is already illegal, because many Americans like to think that our laws reflect our nation's commitment to equality. However, those working for lesbian, gay, bisexual and transgender equity see clearly that a decidedly different reality is reflected in our federal laws. Sadly, it is a worldview, sometimes connected to a moral code, that says to those who are lesbian, gay, bisexual or transgender that their identities are unworthy of protection from discrimination and that their families are unworthy of equality.

Indeed, there is currently no federal protection from discrimination based on sexual orientation. The lack of federal protections carries dangerous implications, suggesting at the very least that it is unnecessary to extend workplace non-discrimination laws to lesbian, gay, bisexual and transgender individuals. At worst, the lack of federal protection further perpetuates bigotry and discrimination, fostering an atmosphere in which companies have the right to fire individuals just for being lesbian, gay, bisexual or transgender. If your boss were, for example, a member of a group that holds a strong position against homosexuality, then merely disclosing that you are lesbian, gay, bisexual and transgender could cost you your job, and in many parts of the country you would have little recourse.

As proposed in 2008, the Employment Non-Discrimination Act passed by the U.S. House of Representatives (but not taken up in the Senate in 2008) excluded protection from discrimination based on gender identity.[13] This omission illustrates the sad reality that transgender individuals face even more resistance and obstacles than lesbian, gay and bisexual individuals do. It also raises important issues regarding the degree to which advocates are cohesively working for equality for all lesbian, gay, bisexual and transgender employees. Omitting protections related to gender identity at the federal level has implications for the workplace, signaling to transgender employees that they are unworthy of the same protections that would be extended to gay employees. Furthermore, many incidents of workplace bullying related to sexual orientation are directed at gender nonconformity. This creates a significant link between protection based on gender identity and working toward establishing a workplace free from bullying and harassment.

In the fall of 2007, with a threat of a filibuster in the Senate and an expected veto from President George W. Bush, the Employment Non-Discrimination Act had little chance of becoming law during the Bush administration. ENDA's slow progress suggests that lesbian, gay, bisexual and transgender individuals enjoy limited public support, because they were unable to gather the necessary votes on Capitol Hill or persuade President Bush to rethink his position. However, to a great extent, public opinion and corporate practice at that time ran counter to government policy. As of mid-2009, a fully inclusive ENDA is expected to be passed by the House and Senate and signed into law by President Barack Obama.

Cultural conservatives benefit from the fact that most people apparently pay little attention, if any, to this battle. Survey results show that 60% of heterosexual adults thought that federal law already protected people from being fired due to sexual orientation. After learning that it is legal to fire someone for being gay or lesbian, 64% said that they believed that to be unfair. In this case, as in many others, there is a gap between public will and political leadership.[14] Those who oppose equality for lesbian, gay, bisexual and transgender individuals are typically vociferous and passionate. They have been successful in creating the impression that they represent a significant mass of voters, although they actually constitute a powerful fringe group.

Public opinion polls regarding transgender employees reveal a higher level of resistance by the general public to transgender rights. In a 2007 national survey conducted by Out & Equal, 67% of all heterosexuals surveyed believed that transgender employees should be evaluated based on their work performance rather than for being transgender. In this same survey, 79% of heterosexual respondents said that lesbian, gay or bisexual employees should be judged based on their work performance rather than their sexual orientation.[15] The twelve-point difference in the findings illustrates the sad reality that those surveyed were more supportive of lesbian, gay, and bisexual employees than of transgender workers.

Without federal protection, lesbian, gay, bisexual and transgender individuals must look to state laws or workplace policies that provide them with protections from discrimination. Currently, 20 states prohibit discrimination based on sexual orientation and 12 of those states also prohibit discrimination based on gender identity.[16] At the time of this writing, states that provide protection based on sexual orientation and gender identity are California, Colorado, Illinois, Iowa, Maine, Minnesota, New Jersey, New Mexico, Oregon, Rhode Island, Vermont, and Washington. States that provide only protection based on sexual orientation are Connecticut, Hawaii, Maryland, Massachusetts, Nevada, New Hampshire, New York, and Wisconsin. As *Allies at Work* goes to press, the other 30 states offer no protection.

Even in companies that provide job security for lesbian, gay, bisexual and transgender individuals, there is still discrimination in the distribution of benefits. Millions of lesbian, gay, bisexual and transgender individuals are denied health care benefits that the spouses of heterosexual employees enjoy. As a result, domestic partner benefits are critically important. Among lesbian, gay, bisexual and transgender adults, 76% rate it as extremely or very important that their company offer equal health benefits to all employees.

However, even well-intentioned employers cannot easily offer health benefits that are exactly equal. Married heterosexual employees may enjoy spousal benefits in terms of health insurance and other benefits, and these employees are not taxed for the cost of their family benefits, which ultimately amounts to additional compensation. However, lesbian and gay employees are taxed for their domestic partner benefits, because the Internal Revenue Service considers domestic partner benefits reportable income.[17] For example, if domestic partner benefits total $20,000 per year for someone in the 25% tax bracket, that person has to pay an additional $5,000 in taxes on what the IRS identifies as additional income. In contrast, married employees do not pay taxes on family benefits. As a result of federal law, heterosexual privilege results in more disposable income for heterosexuals, even in companies that have more equitable policies. Even if your company has equitable policies in place, your lesbian, gay, bisexual and transgender colleagues experience discrimination every time they receive a paycheck.

The national media regularly report about the controversy related to same-sex marriage. While a number of states have recently passed laws and state constitutional amendments banning same-sex marriage, a growing number of heterosexual adults believe in extending many of the same rights and benefits of marriage to gay and lesbian couples. For example, 49% of heterosexuals believe that all employees should enjoy the same benefits on the job regardless of sexual orientation. Furthermore, 64% of heterosexuals believe that family and medical leave should apply equally to heterosexual and gay employees. Among heterosexuals, 56% believe that gay and lesbian employees should receive the same family assistance as heterosexual employees when being transferred.[18] It is evident that there's a disconnect between public opinion and corporate policy and practice at this time.

Corporate Matters

The general public has been far more supportive of lesbian, gay, bisexual and transgender individual rights than has the typical elected official. The positions taken by America's corporate leaders also merit examination. Corporations are increasingly demonstrating their support for lesbian, gay, bisexual and transgender employees. This support is the result of courage, hard work, personal risk and advocacy by those who are lesbian, gay, bisexual and transgender, and their allies. We can see these gains within prominent corporations.

Here's a case in point. Until 1996, Procter & Gamble would not permit the formation of a lesbian, gay, bisexual and transgender Employee Resource Group. In 1998, children of same-sex parents were not even allowed to attend a company-sponsored family function at a local amusement park.[19] Employees received a clear message that if they were lesbian, gay, bisexual or transgender, they'd better leave that identity at home. At work, each of these individuals needed to spend energy hiding details about their lives. Former Proctor & Gamble employee Heidi Green, now Co-chair of Out & Equal's San Francisco Bay Area Regional Affiliate, remembers the situation vividly: "That fear of revealing who I was, particularly at work. I had a boss who suspected I was a lesbian, and I tried to hide it. I was one of those people who didn't use pronouns and thought no one could tell. And the thing I realized was that it was so disruptive of my work that I was thinking more about *that* than I was about work. And that frustrated me a lot." Procter & Gamble, like many other Fortune 500 companies, eventually realized that their policies were counterproductive and at odds with their goals of fostering an efficient, productive workforce and also becoming an employer-of-choice. Heidi decided to begin reaching out to her co-workers. They formed an Employee Resource Group, GABLE, with support from the company and from people involved in ERGs at Nestle and Disney. Heidi and a group of local leaders brought Out & Equal's 2001 Workplace Summit to the Cincinnati area to highlight the needs of lesbian, gay, bisexual and transgender employees. Partly as a result, Procter & Gamble announced their inclusion of domestic partner benefits at the 2001 event.

In 2004, Procter & Gamble donated $10,000 for a ballot initiative in Cincinnati that would help ensure equal protection for lesbian, gay, bisexual and transgender individuals. The corporation supported this measure despite the fact that some conservative groups opposing homosexuality organized a boycott of the company's products.[20] By 2009, Procter & Gamble received a nearly perfect score on the CEI, a rating that means many of the company's policies are inclusive of lesbian, gay, bisexual and transgender people.[21] Within one decade, the workplace environment progressed from adversarial to one of advocacy.

Procter & Gamble's growth had parallels elsewhere in corporate America. When Out & Equal was formed in 1998, according to the organization's founder, Selisse Berry, "Five percent of companies were voluntarily putting sexual orientation in their EEO policies. No one was talking about gender identity and expression. Now a staggering 98% of the world's largest employers put sexual orientation in their EEO policies, and 40% have gender identity and expression."[22]

Not long ago, negative views of lesbian, gay, bisexual and transgender individuals permeated most corporations. Mike Syers, a 42-year-old partner at Ernst & Young, said that when he was younger, he lost his best friend when Mike disclosed his sexual orientation. As a result, during the early stages of his career, Mike never came out at work. Reflecting on opportunities for career advancement, he noted, "I really didn't think there was a long-term career opportunity for me. Being a gay man, I didn't see gay partners."[23]

Hiring and Retaining Top Talent

Hayward Bell, chief diversity officer for Raytheon, explains, "Over the next ten years we're going to need anywhere from 30,000 to 40,000 new employees. We can't afford to turn our back on the talent pool."[24] Ed Offshack, a chemical engineer and gay activist at Procter & Gamble, connects corporate support for lesbian, gay, bisexual and transgender employees with the demands that drive business, including the need to develop the most talented staff: "It's a logic-based community."[25] Many corporations support lesbian, gay, bisexual and transgender workers in order to grow as a business and increase profits.

The corporation and the employee have a common goal: a financial one. It is estimated that nearly 40% of employee compensation is met through the benefits package.[26] If a company's competitor offers domestic partner benefits, then there is pressure to offer the same benefits just to attract and retain the most talented workforce possible. It can cost a company six figures to lose a high-level executive or manager to a competitor. Demonstrating leadership regarding lesbian, gay, bisexual and transgender equality maximizes a corporation's competitive position in the market.

While there has been improvement, support for lesbian, gay, bisexual and transgender employees is not without controversy. Walgreens, for example, donated $100,000 to the 2006 Gay Games. A Walgreens store manager quit in protest, and the company's chief executive received 250,000 protesting emails, most of them organized by a right-wing group. Walgreens, despite the protest, felt that it was important to send a message to their lesbian, gay, bisexual and transgender customers and employees that they were supportive. The company did not waver in its support for the Gay Games.

Of course, companies do not like controversy. Corporations enter a contentious social and political area primarily because it is in their best economic interest to do so. Corporate philanthropy, salary and benefits are business decisions, aimed in part at helping the company position itself as an employer-of-choice. Executives have a responsibility to address the bottom line and maximize profits, which includes having the most talented, productive workforce possible.

Joe Solmonese, president of the Human Rights Campaign, notes that corporations have adjusted their policies and culture to remain competitive: "More businesses than ever before have recognized the value of a diverse and dedicated workforce. More importantly, these employers understand that discrimination against GLBT workers will ultimately hurt their ability to compete in the global marketplace."[27]

In 2009, 259 United States businesses earned a score of 100% on the Corporate Equality Index,* a tool that measures the degree to which a company offers equitable support for lesbian, gay, bisexual and transgender employees. That number is a 33% increase over 2008. As recently as 2002, only 13 companies qualified for the 100% score. Today, 9 million American workers are employed at companies that have earned a perfect score on the Corporate Equality Index.[28]

Many companies are working to improve or maintain their rating on diversity scorecards. Perhaps even more telling is that the higher a company is ranked by *Fortune* magazine, the higher their

---

*It is also critical to note that there is debate among lesbian, gay, bisexual and transgender workers as to whether the Corporate Equality Index criterion is rigorous enough, particularly concerning gender identity and expression. The Corporate Equality Index is continually reevaluated and revised to require more rigorous criteria for obtaining a perfect score.

Corporate Equality Index ranking is likely to be. For example, among *Fortune*'s top 10 companies:

- 90% prohibit discrimination based on sexual orientation.
- 80% offer domestic partner health benefits.
- 50% prohibit discrimination based on gender identity.[29]

The hateful statements by the president of the American Family Association and the Internet site quoted at the start of this chapter clearly show the active campaign being waged against social and legal equity for lesbian, gay, bisexual and transgender individuals. At the same time, corporations are working for every possible competitive advantage. As companies do so, an increasing number of them have determined that it's good business to be lesbian, gay, bisexual and transgender-friendly.

Hewlett-Packard (HP) has paid attention to this market sector and was one of the nation's first major corporations to establish an Employee Resource Group for lesbian, gay, bisexual and transgender workers and adopt EEO policies prohibiting discrimination on the basis of sexual orientation. "A couple of years ago, as we tried to begin cracking the code for marketing to lesbians, gays, bisexuals and transgender people, we realized we did not have any approved gay or lesbian images in the HP library," says Greg Nika, a global program manager with the company. "Within HP, all of the images that we use have to be in an approved image library. So our previous chief marketing officer worked with our corporate office, and they did a gay and lesbian photo shoot. Now we have lifestyle images of gay and lesbian couples, groups of gay and lesbian people and gay and lesbian couples with kids in different home settings, both using HP products and in general day-to-day activities. We also have an internal pride logo that is brand compliant, and we have a corporate team that is really starting to come to us proactively when they get opportunities to market to the gay and lesbian community… We have a lot more work to do, but we have all the building blocks in place."[30]

Advances at HP that have won awards from Out & Equal include the 2003 addition of gender identity and expression to the company's Nondiscrimination and Harassment-Free Work Environment Policies and the 2008 development of a global council and executive advisory board for the company's LGBT Employee Resource Group. "Now what you see is business people looking at not only how to make their work environments more equitable, but how to take that equity to drive performance," says Adam Wolf, a district manager at HP. "A lot of our competitors and a lot of our business partners are moving the bar up... There's always a goal to reach, and it just keeps us motivated because we want everyone to feel so comfortable and so accepted at work that they can really come and be their authentic selves."[31]

Some companies strategically choose not to complete an external LGBT scorecard. One human resources diversity director for a non-participating company explained to me that her CEO refuses to participate in a survey because he does not want to attract protestors by being lesbian, gay, bisexual and transgender-friendly. But even in cases like this, anti-gay and anti-transgender pressure groups may not be having as much impact on companies as they assume. For example, this CEO decided not to fill out a survey, but he still made sure that his company was adhering to the best diversity practices identified in the survey.[32] He believed in the criteria, but felt that getting attention for being lesbian, gay, bisexual and transgender-friendly would be counterproductive to his company's business priorities.

Today, the information superhighway allows online meetings and communication among company employees at job sites located all over the world.[33] Company borders often extend beyond U.S. borders. IBM, a U.S. leader in corporate support for lesbian, gay, bisexual and transgender rights groups, has 23 lesbian, gay, bisexual and transgender Employee Resource Groups around the globe, including in Singapore, Slovakia and Colombia. IBM provides this support network despite the fact that in 80 countries, homosexuality or homosexual sex remains illegal.[34]

Taking lesbian, gay, bisexual and transgender support a step further, Microsoft has even entered the political arena and lobbied the state of Washington to ban discrimination based on sexual orientation. CEO Steve Ballmer explained, "Diversity in the workplace is such an important issue for our businesses that it should be included in our legislative agenda."[35]

In the United States, the opposition to lesbian, gay, bisexual and transgender rights is real, but not nearly as strong as many politicians perceive it to be. However, this perception has left federal law lagging behind what has become customary corporate policy. Public opinion polls and Fortune 500 policies demonstrate a shift toward greater support for lesbian, gay, bisexual and transgender individuals.

The 5 P's: Protection, Progress, Procurement, Pride, Productivity

It is important to identify ways in which we can build a workplace culture of equity for all employees. To that end, I have created the 5 P's for workplace productivity (see Figure 2.2). This pyramid provides a tool for examining how the right corporate culture helps ensure a highly productive and loyal workforce.

A primary objective for any corporation is to maximize productivity. A productive workforce fosters stronger corporate results and greater corporate benefits; employees manage their time efficiently. A productive workforce results in part from visionary, inspirational and responsive corporate leadership. There are specific steps that a company can take to ensure strong worker productivity among lesbian, gay, bisexual and transgender employees and their allies.

At the base of the 5 P's, as seen in Figure 2.2, is **Protection**. The base of a productive workforce originates from nondiscrimination policies and equal benefits. These benefits will be more closely examined in a later chapter, but briefly they include creation and support of Employee Resource Groups/Affinity Groups, providing domestic partner benefits (including family leave, medical leave, bereavement leave, and other associated benefits), and inclusion of sexual orientation and gender identity/expression in company non-discrimination policies. Specific transgender benefits should include mental health counseling, hormone therapy, medical visits, surgical procedures, and short-term disability after surgical procedures.

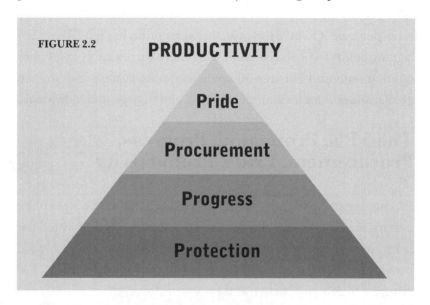

FIGURE 2.2

PRODUCTIVITY

Pride

Procurement

Progress

Protection

The next step in the hierarchy is **Progress.** Progress is the goal of gradual or even rapid betterment for the corporation. This is arguably the most challenging step, as it requires working to change corporate culture. Creating cultural change often entails mandatory diversity training to give staff accurate information about sexual orientation and gender identity/expression and foster insight into relevant diversity issues. In addition, companies have found that mandatory AIDS education supports diversity goals and helps reduce homophobia by correcting misinformation about homosexuality and

HIV transmission. Staff trainings should provide affective, cognitive and behavioral changes that focus on organizational culture to maximize workplace productivity.

"Today's business leaders are looking for training that helps shape their planning and future," says Patricia Baillie, Out & Equal's training and professional development manager. "It is vital we deliver cost-effective, comprehensive training that can reach all their employees. With training, management can impart the concepts, metrics and personal stories to advance true LGBT workplace equality."

Progress is an ongoing, fluid goal that requires constant monitoring and adjusting. Corporations earn a reputation as employers-of-choice when they dedicate themselves to gradual betterment of corporate culture. This means providing equal protection in company policies and benefits and developing a workplace culture that fosters a positive work environment. Once basic protections are provided, perhaps no issue is more pertinent than **Progress**, because changing the corporate culture allows a company to become an employer-of-choice. Allies play an essential role in working for corporate progress. Their role in training and development will be more closely examined in a later chapter.

Progress leads to confidence in the workplace and a greater capacity for **Procurement** of the most talented workforce. Lesbian, gay, bisexual and transgender employees working in supportive environments let their friends and professional colleagues know about their company's positive approach. In some instances, they enter their companies' names for awards, such as the Out & Equal Workplace Awards, or otherwise shower their employers with accolades at corporate diversity and professional conferences. As a result, company diversity efforts pay off by enhancing a company's reputation and position as an employer-of-choice for lesbian, gay, bisexual and transgender individuals and their allies. The company's ability to retain and also procure workforce talent is strengthened.

The result will be increased workplace **Pride,** creating a loyal and motivated workforce dedicated to higher productivity to ensure a strong and competitive work environmnt.

Allies Surveyed on an Inclusive Work Environment

Let's examine how heterosexual coworkers, allies and potential allies, view diversity and inclusion in respect to sexual orientation and gender identity.

An overwhelming majority of heterosexuals, 88%, would feel either positive or indifferent if they learned that a co-worker is lesbian or gay. In contrast, 12% would feel negatively about the person.[36] While this shows high rates of acceptance or at least indifference, the 12% number is understandably disheartening for lesbian, gay, bisexual and transgender individuals. A person who possesses negative feelings could be a direct supervisor or even the CEO. The risk of coming out on the job increases significantly if there is little or no support network in the workplace. Allies are critical in creating and fostering this support network, and they can do so without risking the personal backlash or rejection so often experienced by lesbian, gay, bisexual and transgender individuals.

In opinion polls, a large majority of heterosexuals report positive or indifferent feelings toward gay coworkers, but the work environment continues to be hostile and even harassing for some lesbian, gay, bisexual and transgender individuals. For example, 51% of lesbian and gay workers have heard anti-gay comments at work, and 15% report having been harassed by their coworkers.[37] For lesbian, gay, bisexual and transgender workers, this too often results in a stressful division between work and personal life. While a solid majority of the American workforce is accepting of lesbian, gay, bisexual and transgender individuals, the small, rejecting minority can have an adverse impact on one's work-life and livelihood.

Lesbian, gay, bisexual and transgender employees understandably fear discrimination. In the United States military, for example, it is policy to fire lesbian and gay patriots who have risked their lives for America. The Pentagon fires two lesbian, gay, bisexual or transgender people every day. Since implementation of the "Don't Ask, Don't Tell" policy, the military has even fired 58 Arabic translators, professionals who are scarce and sorely needed by the U.S. military in Iraq and Afghanistan.[38] More than 12,000 enlisted men and women have been discharged from the military since the 1994 enactment of the policy. Randy Foster, a former Navy Air Force Captain, lied about being gay while serving in the United States military. Eventually tired of hiding his identity, he left the military for the private sector. The skills that he developed in the military building observation satellites now benefit his new employer, IBM. He explained his decision to leave the military: "Come hell or high water, I wanted to live one life. The only thing I have to hide now are national security secrets, and those are good secrets."[39]

Among lesbian, gay, bisexual and transgender adults, 67% consider it extremely or very important that there be a written non-discrimination policy inclusive of sexual orientation.[40] Without such a policy, employees are understandably hesitant to come out of the closet, and this situation makes them less likely to contribute at their highest level of productivity.

For most, coming out is a multi-faceted and ongoing process. Individuals often come out of the closet in stages, depending on the trust and intimacy that they have developed with those around them. Those who identify as gay are most likely to come out to their friends (92%). Additional groups, listed in descending order, include their parents (78%), grandparents or cousins (68%), and acquaintances or casual friends (68%). The lowest comfort level measured in this study involved coming out to colleagues at work (66%). While it is encouraging to see that a majority of self-identified lesbian, gay, bisexual and transgender employees are out at work, almost one-third who are out to friends are not out at work.[41]

The implication is that there is significant work necessary to ensure greater comfort and equity at work. Indeed, lesbian, gay, bisexual and transgender individuals have a long list of good reasons for not coming out. For example, 54% cite concern about becoming the victim of a hate crime. Rejection by families is a concern for 39% of individuals surveyed, and rejection by friends is a concern for 32%. Over one-quarter of lesbian, gay, bisexual and transgender individuals fear losing their jobs.[42] It is reasonable to assume that most of those who reported fearing job loss are located in states and workplaces that lack nondiscrimination policies inclusive of sexual orientation and gender identity.

Mark Shields of the Human Rights Campaign's Coming Out Project notes that 70% of heterosexuals state that they know someone who is lesbian, gay, bisexual or transgender. This shows that today it is more common to self-disclose one's sexual orientation or gender identity. Shields's comments are a reminder that changing corporate culture is a process and there is a need for a company to **Progress** in adjusting its work culture: "For most people, coming out or opening up to someone starts with a conversation. And for those interested in fostering strong, deep relationships with their friends and family, living openly often allows for closer relationships with the people they care about most."[43]

People who are out to friends and family are often ready to acknowledge their sexual orientation the work world. In 2007, 64% of gay employees were comfortable introducing their significant other to their coworkers, while in 2002, only 50% were comfortable doing so. When it comes to putting a picture of a significant other on an office desk or wall, 54% of gay employees were comfortable doing so in 2007. Only 34% were comfortable doing so in 2002. It is encouraging that this research demonstrates an increased level of comfort. However, the levels of discomfort are unacceptably high when one considers that it is the expected norm for heterosexual employees to not just display pictures but also refer to or discuss their families and relationships.[44]

However, family matters can sometimes be a prompt for lesbian, gay, bisexual and transgender individuals to disclose their orientation. For example, Mike Syers, the business partner at Ernst & Young who was reluctant to come out because he knew no other gay executives, decided to self-disclose when he and his partner adopted a daughter. This change in his family impelled him to come out: "I will never, ever let her think that her family is something to be ashamed of." When he disclosed his sexual orientation to a colleague, she was accepting and seemingly unfazed.[45]

Sadly, not every lesbian, gay, bisexual or transgender individual receives a positive or neutral response when coming out to co-workers. Individual reluctance to disclose sexual orientation or gender identity/expression at work may often relate to messages and values in the larger society regarding lesbian, gay, bisexual and transgender people. The reality is that openly sharing that one is lesbian, gay, bisexual or transgender can lead to facing not just tension but even perfectly legal discrimination.

Family Matters

At the time of this writing, Connecticut, Iowa, Maine, Massachusetts, New Hampshire and Vermont recognize same-sex marriage. Just six other states* give full or partial recognition to same-sex relationships.[46] California recognizes marriage equality only for the 18,000 same-sex marriages that took place in the state in 2008; the broader

---

*The following states provide the equivalent of state-level spousal rights to same sex couples through civil unions or domestic partnerships: California, New Jersey and Oregon. The following provide some spousal rights: District of Columbia, Hawaii, Maine and Washington state.

issue of marriage equality continues to be a matter of public and legal debate there. In May 2008, same-sex marriage became legal in California when the state's Supreme Court ruled that the right to marry was a basic civil right guaranteed to all state citizens, regardless of sexual orientation. Over 18,000 gay and lesbian couples wed. Later that year, California voters narrowly approved Proposition 8, a ballot initiative which amended the state constitution with the declaration that only marriage between a man and a woman would be valid or recognized. This eliminated same-sex couples' right to marry and raised questions about the legal status of those who had married during the previous five months.[47] In 2009, the California Supreme Court upheld Proposition 8 and, at the same time, declared the existing 18,000 marriages to be valid. The state's battle over the issue is expected to continue through further electoral and legal challenges, because of the strongly held positions on both sides and the increasing support for marriage equality among younger voters, who over time will make up a greater percentage of the electorate.

Fear over disclosing that a same-sex couple is raising a child is well-founded, because many state laws fail to offer protections for gay and lesbian parents. Coping with discriminatory family laws is stressful and requires the investment of a significant amount of energy. It also requires an economic investment, including attorney fees, to establish rights such as inheritance and other legal rights conferred by marriage.

In some states, such as Florida, same-sex couples are denied the right to adopt children. The case of one Florida couple powerfully illustrates the pain of this discriminatory law. Perhaps even more distressing, this law's bigoted foundation inflicts emotional wounds upon some of society's most vulnerable: foster children.

Steven Lofton and his partner of 20 years, Roger Croteau, were foster parents and had been raising John Roe as their son since he was placed in foster care with them as an infant. John went to school daily, was on the swim team, and came home to homework, chores and family dinner. Lofton and Croteau also became foster parents to two other infants, Franke and Tracy, whom they raised into their later teens. John, Franke and Tracy all think of each other as siblings.

Steven Lofton became a licensed foster parent in 1988 in order to take care of HIV-positive infants who had been abandoned. Over the years, he has been a foster parent to eight children with HIV/AIDS. Due to the demanding nature of caring for HIV positive children, the State of Florida insisted that Lofton give up his career as a pediatric AIDS nurse and that he care for his foster children full-time. Lofton agreed, giving up his career to dedicate himself full-time to his HIV-positive foster care children. In 1998, the agency that placed the children with Lofton and Croteau created an award for outstanding foster parent of the year. The first award was given to Lofton and Croteau, and it was then named after them: the "Lofton-Croteau Award."

Florida eventually terminated John Roe's biological parents' parental rights, making him eligible to be adopted. Originally, the State of Florida asked Lofton if he wanted to adopt John. He did and filed an adoption application. However, during the 1970s, Florida had passed a law stating that, "No person eligible to adopt under this statute may adopt if that person is a homosexual." As a result, Lofton's application to adopt John was denied. Lofton and his partner, who had been publicly recognized as outstanding foster parents and role models, could not qualify to continue to care for John. Lofton then received a phone call from John's caseworker, who told him she was looking for someone else to adopt John. She callously asked Lofton if he knew anyone who might be interested.

Lofton sued, saying that the Florida law violated the Equal Protection Clause of the Fourteenth Amendment of the United States Constitution. He charged that Florida's law violated the right to equal protection not just for the lesbians and gay men who seek to adopt but also for the children being raised by lesbian and gay caregivers. He argued that the law was unconstitutional.

Unfortunately, Florida did not agree. The State argued that the law has two rational reasons. First, it has an interest in expressing moral disapproval of "homosexual households." Second, it believes that it is promoting the best interests of children by placing them with married mothers and fathers, whom the State asserts make better parents. Although Florida was unable to provide any evidence linking heterosexuality to inherently better parenting, it argued that the United States Constitution allows it to base the law on mere speculation. The federal circuit court upheld the Florida law, and the United States Supreme Court decided not to hear the case.

Furthermore, in the Florida courts, a gay or lesbian parent divorcing an opposite-sex partner or fighting for visitation rights may find his or her own sexual orientation put on trial. The Florida laws are clearly a moral violation, though evidently not a legal violation, of human rights. While the Lofton story serves as a powerful case study, discriminatory family laws are found outside Florida's borders.

In 2005, Alabama Supreme Court Justice Roy Moore explained his rationale for discriminating against gay and lesbian parents: "The effect of such a lifestyle upon children must not be ignored, and the lifestyle should never be tolerated.... Any person who engages in such conduct is presumptively unfit to have custody of minor children under the established laws of the state."[48] In Kentucky, the courts have awarded a change in custody based on the sexual orientation of a parent, arguing that the child's lesbian mother could endanger the child.[49]

These are not isolated examples. There is a widespread lack of protection for lesbian, gay, bisexual and transgender families. Today, approximately 250,000 American children are being raised by same-sex couples. Only about half the states allow adoption by an unmarried second partner.[50] In some cases, a state law permits and even advocates discrimination against lesbian, gay, bisexual and transgender parents. These laws are based on the view that heterosexuality is morally superior to homosexuality. This deeply held bias is being challenged in various parts of society, leading to personal challenges and sometimes conflict for those who are willing to confront this bias.

While the Florida legislature and other discriminatory state officials see little reason to change their laws and keep pace with society, most large corporations have a more sophisticated understanding of what is in the best interest of a strong and effective workplace culture. Companies work diligently to assure their employees that they are valued members of the team. Clearly, the culture war being fought in the political arena has been largely rejected by America's economic leaders.

The contrast is not just stark but also deeply disturbing when we consider the best interests of our society. Many corporations, mindful of the bottom line, are working hard to create a more equitable work environment for all of their employees. Meanwhile, too many of our elected officials fail to show equal leadership in fostering healthy families and communities. Without adequate protection, too many families have to invest their energies in defending their identity, and these investments come at a significant economic and emotional cost, often at the expense of other needs and priorities. It is critical to understand that corporate matters and family matters are not and cannot be mutually exclusive. Job life and home life affect each other. Dealing with a system of laws that discriminates against your family can be stressful and exhausting, and it is difficult to check those feelings of frustration, humiliation and anger at the workplace entrance every day. That is why some corporations are taking positions on public policy issues impacting lesbian, gay, bisexual and transgender individuals and families. They have realized that family law has a direct impact on workplace productivity.

David M. Hall

Lesbian, gay, bisexual and transgender individuals can often remain an invisible minority. The process of coming out, publicly disclosing one's sexual orientation or gender identity/expression, is decidedly different from the experiences of virtually any other, more visible minority. Increasing awareness of the larger conflicts within our culture has prompted many employers to examine what they can do to develop a supportive and accepting atmosphere for their employees. To create such an environment, it is necessary to understand the social climate surrounding the worksite and to fully comprehend the particular challenges of disclosing that one is lesbian, gay, bisexual or transgender in a heterosexist and sometimes viciously homophobic society. Allies have a pivotal role to play in promoting fairness and changing corporate culture.

CHAPTER THREE

"I Think I'm Gay":
Coming Out to Yourself and Others

To comprehend the challenges facing those who consider coming out in the workplace, we need to understand the dynamics of coming out and develop an appreciation of how these dynamics play out in the lives of people who are lesbian, gay, bisexual or transgender. This understanding helps correct the mistaken assumption that a coworker's self-disclosure process only affects the person coming out. In fact, coming out, as well as staying in the closet, affects the corporate environment. This chapter introduces a paradigm developed by a social scientist and applies it to the workplace, so that we can see the effect of the coming out process both on the individual who is coming out and on the company. In doing so, we will begin to understand how allies in the workplace can help someone struggling with the impact of his or her coming out.

There are significant challenges and risks associated with coming out in the workplace. Imagine how it would feel to be a closeted lesbian at work and being constantly asked if you have a boyfriend or having colleagues try to set you up with single male coworkers. For someone who is lesbian, gay or bisexual, disclosing his or her sexual orientation might reduce or eliminate such awkward experiences, but disclosure brings its own risks and challenges.

It is critical that executives, managers, coworkers and allies better identify some of the challenges faced by their lesbian, gay, bisexual and transgender colleagues. This chapter examines the stages that many individuals go through when they come out. The next chapter

David M. Hall

will examine the related issue of the range of responses individuals receive when they come out.

FIGURE 3.1

Tips for Success: The Journey of Coming Out

1. **There are many stages in coming out.** There is no cookie-cutter approach for supporting people in coming out. Individual personalities, combined with different stages of coming out, create varying needs for support.
2. **There are significant differences based on being lesbian, gay, bisexual or transgender.** Know that each individual may have significantly different experiences based on sexual orientation or gender identity.
3. **Create an environment that meets the diverse needs of individuals.** Colleagues who are just coming out may have different needs from the company than those who have been out for a long time and/or are at a later stage in their career. The Cass Identity Model helps identify diverse needs based on developmental stages.
4. **Provide clear signals that you are an ally.** The process of coming out can have a negative impact on workplace productivity. Making it clear that you are an ally can make the coming out process at work easier when an individual is ready to take advantage of the space provided.

The Cass Identity Model: Six Developmental Stages

Researcher Vivian Cass developed a highly regarded Identity Model that frames coming out as six distinct stages. Cass created this model to identify stages of sexual orientation, but for purposes of this book Cass's model can be applied to gender identity/expression as well.* It must be clearly stated that these stages have no relationship to a person's age or level of maturity. In fact, individuals report going through these stages at various ages.

Additionally, not all individuals experience every stage, and some of the stages are experienced in decidedly different ways. These differences may have to do with whether the experiences are based on sexual orientation or gender identity/expression. The differences are also dependent on factors such as biological sex, cultural norms, individual personalities and other variables.

The six stages identified by Cass and closely examined throughout this chapter are:

1. Identity Confusion
2. Identity Comparison
3. Identity Tolerance
4. Identity Acceptance
5. Identity Pride
6. Identity Synthesis[51]

It should be stressed that no stage is inherently more evolved or mature than another. These stages should not be thought of as a hierarchy but, instead, as responses appropriately fitting a person's needs depending on his or her unique circumstances. It should also be noted that individuals may have fluid rather than consecutive movement between these stages. For example, there are good reasons that individuals may move from Identity Pride to Identity Synthesis and then later return to Identity Pride.

---

*It should be noted that there are a variety of models that can be used as a framework for both sexual orientation and gender identity. Cass's model was chosen because it is easily applicable to the workplace.

Most children grow up assuming heterosexuality to be an innate characteristic in others as well as themselves. The assumption originates in adults, who often teach and reinforce this expectation. For example, when my wife was pregnant with our first child, the ultrasound revealed that we were expecting a girl. One person, noting that a family friend was having a boy, said, "When they get older, they can go out." The person assumed that my daughter was heterosexual before she was even born. Since the time my daughter was just a toddler, people have told me how beautiful she is and often followed this remark with clichés such as, "You're going to need to keep the boys away with a shotgun." Sometimes I hear these assumptions from people I consider to be allies on lesbian, gay, bisexual and transgender issues. I can't help but reflect that these comments demonstrate the degree to which some well-meaning allies unwittingly reinforce the assumptions and enforcement of heterosexuality. Imagine a young man attracted to the same sex but constantly asked about his girlfriend. When he fields such questions, he is being reminded that his feelings conflict with the relationship expectations of those around him. He does not want to disappoint his loved ones, yet he knows that he feels differently than everyone else seems to assume he should. Being routinely misperceived motivates lesbian, gay, bisexual and transgender individuals to come out.

The Cass model provides a helpful framework for identifying some of the challenges of being lesbian, gay, bisexual or transgender in a heterosexist world. The day-to-day challenges may be significant or small, but these are trials that heterosexuals never have to consider in their personal and professional lives. Heterosexuality allows an individual to ignore or remain unaware of the conflict that is created by the near-universal assumption of heterosexuality. Careful examination of the Cass model and the assumption of heterosexuality is critical in creating an equitable work environment.

I have created a guiding question for each Cass Identity Stage to make the model accessible and easily applicable for use in the workplace.

FIGURE 3.2

Stage #	Cass identity stage	Guiding question
1	Identity confusion	Am i gay?
2	Identity comparison	What does this mean?
3	Identity tolerance	Are there others?
4	Identity acceptance	Where is my support network?
5	Identity pride	Whom do i tell?
6	Identity synthesis	So what?

The way in which a person goes through these stages is strongly influenced by the messages and attitudes expressed by those around her and by the larger society toward lesbian, gay, bisexual and transgender individuals. The workplace is one of many environments that can have a significant impact on how a person experiences and manages these stages.

Identity Confusion Stage

Stage One: Identity Confusion involves someone who is lesbian, gay, bisexual or transgender reconciling the fact that his or her identity does not fit with conventional beliefs about sexual orientation or gender identity/expression. In this stage, individuals wonder whether they are lesbian, gay, bisexual or transgender. The ways in which they manage this question have varying results from one individual to the next. Individuals can move toward a path of self-acceptance, self-denial or self-rejection.

How an individual manages the difficulties of being lesbian, gay, bisexual, or transgender in a heterosexist world can lead in decidedly different directions. Acceptance may lead to coming out and possibly advocating for lesbian, gay, bisexual and transgender rights and issues. Rejection may result in enrolling in aversion therapy

programs in an attempt to become an ex-gay.* Those who pursue
this option are less likely to leave this stage.

For example, Pastor Ted Haggard was president of the National
Association of Evangelicals. Married, with children, Haggard often
preached about the sins of homosexuality. It was later revealed that
Haggard was sexually active with a gay male prostitute.[52] He then
resigned from his leadership positions in his church and with the
National Association of Evangelicals and went into counseling.

Research provides correlating data about the relationship of
self-rejection during Identity Confusion and the ways in which
that person may perpetuate bias toward lesbian, gay, bisexual and
transgender people. This research measures not only attitudes
toward homosexuality but also sexual arousal, and is not at first
glance workplace-related, but the study's findings have workplace
implications. Indeed, the research connects an individual's same-sex
attraction with overcompensating in his rejecting attitude to mask
his true identity in an attempt to avoid being perceived as gay.

Dr. Henry Adams, a psychologist at the University of Georgia,
conducted a study that sheds light on the motivations of some men
who are homophobic or heterosexist. In this study, he provided
psychological tests to male college students. Based on the results, he
divided the participants into groups that were categorized as homophobic and non-homophobic. After the survey, study participants
were physically connected to a penile plethysmograph to measure
their sexual arousal. The participants then watched sexually explicit
heterosexual, lesbian and gay films. The men rated as homophobic
according to Adams's classification were significantly less aroused
by the sexually explicit heterosexual films than were the men in the

*Ex-gay is someone who identified as lesbian or gay and currently identifies as het-
erosexual. The ex-gay movement is led mainly by anti-gay ideological groups which
promote programs to "convert" homosexuals to heterosexuality. The American
Psychological Association does not categorize homosexuality as a mental disorder;
it has created guidelines to protect individuals from abuses in "aversion therapy,"
"conversion therapy" and "reparative therapy."

40 "I Think I'm Gay"

non-homophobic group. Additionally, the sexually explicit gay films resulted in a 34% arousal rate for non-homophobic participants and an overwhelming 80% arousal rate for homophobic participants.[53]

This research confirms that homophobia is often associated with repressed homosexual desires. What Adams's work suggests is that those who adamantly oppose equity for lesbian, gay, bisexual and transgender individuals in the workplace may be struggling with their own suppressed same-sex attraction and feelings. Their opposition and hostility may actually be a veiled attempt to hide their orientation or identity in an effort to ensure their own self-protection. Adams's research has implications that help explain some of the struggles that lesbian, gay, bisexual and transgender individuals face in self-acceptance, as well as some of the hidden motivations behind much of the bigotry they encounter. It is important to consider how Identity Confusion can impact the work environment. If an executive or manager were lesbian, gay, bisexual or transgender in the Identity Confusion stage and responded with self-rejection or denial, what impact would that have on the work environment? What issues might exist for them not just related to championing but even to supporting lesbian, gay, bisexual and transgender issues in the workplace? In some workplaces, lesbian, gay, bisexual and transgender employees might experience the greatest resistance to equality from closeted lesbian, gay, bisexual and transgender co-workers, managers and executives. Open acceptance of workplace equity could feel risky to those who have worked so diligently to hide themselves away. Henry Adams's research suggests that people who are self-rejecting during the Identity Confusion stage believe that they have little to gain and much to lose if they support workplace equity. Their motivation is not so much fear of other people who are lesbian, gay, bisexual, or transgender as it is fear of the self. They cannot reconcile themselves with who they are and therefore have a decidedly higher level of motivation for resisting workplace equity.

Identity Confusion Case Study   Phillip and Rosita dated in college and moved in together after graduation. Phillip has a tough and demanding job. However, he comes home to Rosita, a woman he just adores. She is beautiful, kind, sensitive—all qualities that he most values in a significant other. However, he cannot reconcile the fact that the feelings he has for Rosita are more like those he might have for a best friend rather than a wife. He has never gotten excited just by looking at her. Despite the fact that Rosita is extremely attractive, it is work for Phillip to get aroused when they are sexually intimate, which he has increasingly tried to avoid. He is certain that he just needs to give the relationship more time. He knows that relationships take work and eventually he will come to experience feelings of passion and intimacy with Rosita.

At work, Phillip has a male coworker whom he keeps noticing. This particular coworker is head-turning attractive. Phillip likes to see him, is slightly nervous to talk with him, and checks himself in the mirror when he expects that their paths will cross. While getting dressed in the morning, Phillip may even think about how he wants to look for this particular coworker. One day the coworker is talking with Phillip and brushes his hand across Phillip's shoulder. Phillip feels a sensation that he has never felt with Rosita. He goes home to Rosita, hoping he can feel the same thing with her. Despite his efforts, he never feels that way. Phillip begins to wonder if he is gay. Whatever the answer to that question, it might not lead to Phillip being open-minded or supportive of workplace equality. Phillip's questions about his own sexual orientation might not only affect his productivity at work; they might lead him to actually oppose equity for lesbian, gay, bisexual and transgender individuals.

Individuals are at their happiest and most productive when they live in a world where their sexual orientation and gender identity/ expression can be genuinely expressed with the same freedom that people in the sexual majority get to express their identity and relationships. During Identity Confusion, individuals know that they can turn to allies for support but are not yet ready to take advantage of the space that has been created. However, during this stage, they may feel fear about talking with lesbian, gay, bisexual and transgender individuals if they do not want others to find out their secret. Talking with allies carries some but considerably less risk than talking with someone who is openly lesbian, gay, bisexual or transgender. Though they are not yet ready to confide in anyone, knowing that allies around them offer a supporting and accepting space provides a powerful message.

If people in your workplace are questioning whether they are lesbian, gay, bisexual or transgender, allies should ask themselves the following questions when evaluating the workplace atmosphere: Has a space been created in which it is okay to express questions or feelings about being lesbian, gay, bisexual or transgender? Have you explicitly made it clear that you are a safe resource, that you are ready to be part of someone's support network? Do others know that they will find support and acceptance from you if they come out or even just disclose their struggle? Have employees been given explicit messages about the corporation's attitudes, whether accepting or rejecting, regarding lesbian, gay, bisexual and transgender personnel? The answers to these questions are likely to have a direct impact on Stage Two of the Cass Model.

Identity Comparison Stage

Stage Two: Identity Comparison is when a person begins to accept being lesbian, gay, bisexual or transgender but also struggles with how to handle this new identity. It is clear that there is rejection and even hatred in the world, so weighing the consequences of coming out often becomes isolating. The implications of being lesbian, gay, bisexual or transgender have not truly been confronted, and an individual now must confront both the loss of heterosexual privilege and the managing of heterosexist discrimination or even homophobic oppression.

Identity Comparison is when individuals begin to consciously confront the possibility that some people may regard them and their relationships as perverse. This is reinforced in a myriad of ways. If you are lesbian, gay, bisexual or transgender, you do not have the same legal rights as your heterosexual peers. You also see few positive representations of yourself in the popular media and the larger society, including corporate executives and elected officials.

Heterosexual readers may not have previously considered how isolating this situation would feel, because the nature of privilege is not to notice it unless forced to. For people going through the stage of Identity Comparison, ignorance ceases to be an option. The nature of heterosexual privilege becomes painfully clear, and the loss of it is something that many closeted lesbian, gay, bisexual and transgender individuals may understandably fear. If you accept that you are lesbian, gay, bisexual or transgender, you accept the loss of both privilege and power within our society.

Selisse Berry, executive director of Out & Equal, reached the Stage of Identity Comparison while at the San Francisco Theological Seminary. At the seminary, she learned that the Presbyterian Church did not ordain lesbians. Selisse realized that there was a conflict between her career path and her personal life that she couldn't easily resolve: "If I was going to be honest and open about my life, it would really be a roadblock to my career path. I talked to a woman who is an out lesbian at a Unitarian Church, and she said, 'How do you plan to talk to people about love, if you can't talk about whom you love?'"[54]

Identity Comparison brings with it concrete questions about how this will impact a person's standing at work and beyond. During this stage, people who are lesbian, gay, bisexual or transgender are likely to ask themselves some of the following questions: How will my coworkers feel? What will my boss think of me? Am I going to lose my job? What will I do during the holiday party? How do I disclose that I will be going through a gender transition? How will my parents, family and neighbors respond? If a person fears rejection or punishment, honest disclosure takes considerable courage and strength.

The fear of rejection or punishment can lead to many individuals at this stage remaining in the closet. The isolation of the closet can have a devastating impact on a person. It can result in depression and self-destructive behaviors. It is natural to withdraw from social networks and work in order to avoid revealing one's true orientation or identity. During Identity Comparison, an individual is likely to struggle to be productive in the workplace. The energy that top performance would require is understandably directed toward protecting oneself. Indeed, working to hide something that is interwoven into the fabric of our lives can consume a considerable amount of energy. The complications of the situation arise from the nature of being an invisible minority. The average workplace—even if it has an overall commitment to diversity—will probably not have considered the needs of employees in this stage, as the associated feelings are far less common for visible minorities.

Identity Comparison Case Study　Phillip realizes that he is gay but doesn't know what to do. There is so much to lose: coworkers, friends, family and livelihood. And what about Rosita?

He feels rejected and isolated. Phillip realizes that he has been living a lie but is only now beginning to confront the implications of his reality. All of his life, he has been trying so hard not to be gay. He becomes depressed, withdrawn. He is not really close with anyone who is gay and fears that he will lose everyone he cares about if he is honest about his feelings and orientation.

He becomes filled with fear at work. He begins to take a longer walk to the bathroom, so that no one will notice him stealing glances at the male coworker he finds attractive. Rosita brings home a purple dress shirt for him, and he refuses to wear it, because it is an atypical color for men to wear. Phillip is guarded in conversation. He keeps himself from engaging in any conversations about topics that would be stereotypically considered gay. There is no one he would dare tell about what he is feeling.

Meanwhile, Phillip is smart and charismatic and has always expected to move up the corporate ladder. The perfect position has finally opened up. Phillip applies for the promotion, but he does not receive it. Having a good relationship with his immediate supervisor, he is told that he will eventually get promoted, but he has shown inconsistent performance lately.

"I don't know what is going on," his supervisor explains, sympathetically. "We are waiting for the old Phillip to come back. Get yourself back on track, and your future is bright in this department."

The presence of a strong support network is not something that people at the Identity Comparison stage are ready to take advantage of. In fact, they may very well continue to keep their distance from people who are a part of a support network out of fear that others will notice. Identity Comparison for some may include a hope that they are not, in fact, lesbian, gay, bisexual and transgender, despite the strong feelings they cannot suppress.

During Identity Comparison, employees cannot maximize their workplace productivity. This is why supporting diversity in the workplace is critical to the company's well-being. Individuals spend different lengths of time during this developmental stage. For some, it is a relatively short period of time, while for others it can be agonizingly long. Support for lesbian, gay, bisexual and transgender employees will create an environment that helps to shorten this stage and allow the individuals to move to a healthier personal space, which then fosters increased workplace productivity.

For people who are transgender, this stage can be even more challenging. Gay workers who move beyond this stage can hide their identities and significant others from their coworkers if they so choose. However, presenting oneself as the other sex cannot be easily masked. Gender and sex transitioning eventually becomes evident, because concealment ceases to be an option. As a result, transgender people may experience a more intense struggle about coming out than do those who are gay. In fact, some transgender individuals find the prospect of rejection and resistance so overwhelming that they choose to move to a new location to carry out their gender transition. Rather than encounter what may be fierce rejection, some choose to start over, severing all ties to their current community.

In some workplaces, allies will have provided silent support through this stage. For example, the ERG may have posted signs about their allies program, and clear statements have been made. These steps may have eased the internal struggle of some lesbian, gay, bisexual and transgender individuals, but at this stage, they have yet to reach out for a support network. However, the environment that has been created will allow lesbian, gay, bisexual and transgender coworkers to come out sooner and find themselves at Cass's later stages in the workplace. Workplace allies contribute to providing a support network that helps create an environment of safety for the next stage, Identity Tolerance.

Identity Tolerance Stage

Stage Three: Identity Tolerance is when a person becomes increasingly familiar with others who are lesbian, gay, bisexual and transgender. In fact, those who are the most isolated may just be beginning to realize that other lesbian, gay, bisexual and transgender people actually exist in their world. Surrounding oneself with lesbian, gay, bisexual and transgender individuals helps break down the walls of

David M. Hall

isolation. Individuals at this stage may visit a lesbian, gay, bisexual and transgender issues website, visit a gay bar, watch gay-themed television programming or engage in other activities that will provide some sort of support. Some may begin to exhibit supposedly stereotypical behavior, which may take the form of atypical gender mannerisms. In the Identity Tolerance stage, individuals may also demonstrate an interest in finding a support network when they experience heterosexism in their work or personal life.

During Identity Tolerance, people begin to look around for signals of whether they can expect acceptance or rejection. They notice whether their boss or coworkers have a rainbow flag or a pink triangle visibly displayed. They take notice of whether the corporation has lesbian, gay, bisexual and transgender executives. Their involvement in their company's Employee Resource Group, provided that one exists, may at this point be limited to anonymous participation in meetings via conference calls.

Identity Tolerance Case Study   Phillip tells Rosita that he has another late night at work. Instead, he goes to a gay bar. He walks inside, feels nervous, and sits at the bar, quickly ordering a drink. He begins to realize how attracted he is to a few men in the club. He has been suppressing these feelings for men for much of his life. He has tried for years to feel this way about women, but without success. As he begins to connect with his feelings for men, he is filled with great fear. To be honest about his sexual orientation will dramatically change his world. He has a great girlfriend and a perfect job, and he loves his friends and family. There is so much to lose, and he is not entirely sure that the potential gains make coming out worthwhile.

This is a stage at which the environment at work can be a critical resource for individuals, particularly if no such environment has been created in employees' personal lives. Becoming familiar with other lesbian, gay, bisexual and transgender individuals provides groundwork for eventually seeking a support network. At this stage, lesbian, gay, bisexual and transgender individuals may begin the process of paying closer attention to the existence of an Employee Resource group, the workplace benefits provided to lesbian, gay, bisexual and transgender employees, company activities during Pride month and other workplace programs. A supportive work environment fosters loyalty among lesbian, gay, bisexual and trans-gender employees and improves the corporation's ability to retain and procure the most talented workforce.

Identity Acceptance Stage

Stage Four: Identity Acceptance involves realizing that it is okay to be lesbian, gay, bisexual or transgender. Here, a support network becomes more important, because this stage involves preparing oneself for possible rejection from the heterosexual community. Even with a strong support network, coming out can still be difficult, though personal and coworker support provides a much more manageable experience when encountering heterosexism. At some point during this stage, individuals begin to openly identify as lesbian, gay, bisexual or transgender

Individuals are beginning to choose to whom they first come out. They are unlikely to select workplace colleagues unless they are also close friends. However, coworkers may find that even if they have a close personal relationship with a lesbian, gay, bisexual or transgender colleague, that person may still be reluctant to disclose his or her sexual orientation or gender identity/expression—out of fear of workplace rejection. It is much more likely for people to share their orientation or identity with a close friend or family member. Eventually, some individuals begin coming out at work during this stage, though data show that this occurs in lower proportion than coming out to family and friends.[55]

Identity Acceptance Case Study After a few months of anonymously participating by phone during his company's Employee Resource Group meetings, Phillip shares his name when he calls in during a meeting, and he is warmly welcomed. The following month, he decides to personally attend the meeting. He is a little surprised to see who is there. He certainly didn't know everyone, but of those he knows casually, there are some whom he had always assumed were heterosexual.

In talking with others at the meeting, he hears some of their coming out stories. Many have a story that is remarkably similar to his own. He feels a huge sense of comfort as he begins to come to the realization that everything, or at least most things, will be okay. However, he asks his coworkers not to tell anyone that he comes to these meetings. It's not that he is embarrassed to be there, he explains. He just wants to come out on his own terms. His colleagues agree, respecting and understanding the individual journey of coming out.

Over the coming months, he discloses that he is gay to Rosita, his family and his friends. He receives a wide variety of responses. As he expected, Rosita is devastated, and he certainly feels immense guilt. She accuses him of lying to her. He explains that he did not fully understand who he truly was, because he was lying to himself. He tells his father, who is surprised but accepting. Phillip's mother, however, is initially decisively rejecting. His brother will not talk to him, though his sisters do not seem to judge him at all. In fact, the only difference in how they treat him is that they sometimes advocate for him. His youngest sister actually wants to set him up with one of her gay friends. Over time, most of his family becomes supportive and accepting, though his brother remains distant and occasionally even hostile.

Phillip eventually starts coming out at work beyond the Employee Resource Group. He doesn't actually say he's gay. He just shares the gender of his date with a few people he trusts when coworkers are talking about their weekends. He doesn't experience any major hostility from his coworkers.

This is the stage at which a supportive work environment can have a critical impact. If a company does not have policies in place—or if they have policies in place but fail to enforce rules meant to ensure equitable treatment of lesbian, gay, bisexual and transgender workers, they risk losing talented employees to more accepting corporate competitors. The business issues addressed in Chapter Two should strongly influence companies to develop and embrace policies that are fully accepting of their lesbian, gay, bisexual and transgender employees. Their own competitive drive should also motivate them to ensure that these policies are being enforced, so that they truly impact corporate culture.

Identity Pride Stage

Stage Five: Identity Pride involves adopting a stronger lesbian, gay, bisexual or transgender identity. The person has now passed the stage of struggling and now has self-acceptance. They fully accept and may even embrace being lesbian, gay, bisexual or transgender. Individuals may feel a responsibility to be openly lesbian, gay, bisexual or transgender in order to serve as a role model or provide a safe space for those who are at an earlier stage. This stage typically involves feelings of lesbian, gay, bisexual and transgender community pride and comfort. Lesbian, gay, bisexual and transgender individuals at this stage may demonstrate an activist approach in their workplace and community. Individuals at the stage of Identity Pride may sit on boards and openly donate to lesbian, gay, bisexual and transgender organizations and causes. They might place a rainbow bumper sticker on their car or on their desk for others to see. They may play a leadership role in their Employee Resource Group—or be instrumental in founding one, if their company lacks this kind of support network. They are a critical resource in the organizational development of a company.

Identity Pride Case Study   A year after Phillip came out, the head of his Employee Resource Group retired. The group asked Phillip if he would take over, and he was honored to do so. Just two months previously, he had put a rainbow flag pin on the board above his desk. He is now dating a male coworker and has a photo of the two of them standing at the Grand Canyon displayed on his desk. Phillip is a member of Parents, Families and Friends of Lesbians and Gays (PFLAG). He attends Out & Equal's annual Summit and was just asked to join the board of the local lesbian, gay, bisexual and transgender youth center.

As the head of his company's Employee Resource Group, Phillip easily recognizes the obstacles to coming out that he experienced. He is passionate about doing what he can to remove those obstacles for others. He knows that they are doing a lot of things correctly at his company, but there are still significant steps to take to become a truly equitable work environment, particularly on transgender issues. In fact, while Phillip wants to see improvement on lesbian, gay, and bisexual issues in the workplace, he feels that transgender issues are about ten years behind in the corporate culture and workplace attitudes.

It can be difficult to fully express oneself during the stage of Identity Pride if one encounters rejection or resistance in the workplace. Sometimes this is an area where there is a disconnect between those who are lesbian, gay, bisexual and people who are transgender. It can be common for a company to have a stronger network of support and acceptance for employees who are lesbian, gay, or bisexual than for those who are transgender. Lesbian, gay, bisexual and transgender Employee Resource Groups may find that they have a number of gay and lesbian members, but no transgender members. This illustrates that lesbian, gay, bisexual and transgender employees may find different degrees of welcome and safety in the work environment.

In the workplace, allies need to recognize the unique perspective of lesbian, gay, bisexual and transgender employees who have reached Identity Pride. They can speak with clarity and conviction to the challenges of working in a heterosexist corporate culture. They can provide invaluable insight into what can be done to ensure that their company establishes an environment that provides lesbian, gay, bisexual and transgender equity.

It should also be noted that there are some individuals who may skip the Identity Pride stage as it is described here. There is a long list of possible reasons. They could be intrinsically quiet or introverted, or they may live in an accepting environment and may not need the same support network that others find valuable. They may be different in style or politics from those who are active in Identity Pride. They may have reached full self-acceptance but do not find that this stage addresses what they are looking for. Their experiences during Identity Pride may be more of a personal journey.

For example, here is how one introverted, brilliant, self-employed gay man, who is also an immigrant, described his decidedly different coming out experience. As a child newly arrived in America, he first learned isolation when he was mocked by his peers as an immigrant. In the family sphere, his religious upbringing taught him that homosexuality was wrong and immoral. For him, Identity Pride and coming out were part of a larger struggle. He explains:

"Being homosexual is a big part of me, and while it defines my worldview to a certain extent, my worldview is more a consequence of the separateness and isolation one feels being homosexual in an intolerant straight society and an immigrant in a foreign country—combined with the conflict of despising the roots of that which you culturally identity with, *i.e.,* being a Catholic.

"When you combine all of these elements, there is a hardening that takes place, and over time you develop a sort of 'f— them all' attitude. This hardening process comes in conjunction with a hypersensitivity toward others whom you see as being similarly isolated and/or segregated.

"I never got into the realm of seeking acceptance from the straight world".[56]

For this person, Identity Pride never included posting a rainbow sticker. Instead, he felt Identity Pride when he fell in love. Describing himself as a "pragmatic isolationist," he quickly moved to the next stage, Identity Synthesis.

Identity Synthesis Stage

Stage 6: Identity Synthesis is a developmental stage that involves a person's sexual orientation as one part of identity, but not as the primary defining quality. The person may still have a strong relationship with the lesbian, gay, bisexual and transgender community, but place a lower level of importance on that community than those who are at Identity Pride.

There are various reasons that this change can occur. Some may find that advocacy gets tiring, and Identity Synthesis allows a person to channel their energy elsewhere. A gay or lesbian couple may have children and have reasons to connect with other young families, perhaps living in suburbia. It should again be stressed that Identity Synthesis is not a more evolved stage than Identity Pride. It is just a stage that meets a different set of individual needs.

Identity Synthesis Case Study   After years of being together, Phillip and his partner get married. This marriage is through their church but is not legally recognized, as they do not live in a state that legally sanctions same-sex marriage. They adopt children and move out of the city and into the suburbs. They are surrounded mainly by heterosexual families, but it is a community in which they seem to enjoy a good amount of acceptance and little if any hostility. Phillip no longer leads his company's Employee Resource Group, though he still attends some of their larger events. He makes relatively large donations to the local lesbian, gay, bisexual and transgender youth center.

He believes that all of those groups played a critical role for him, but now he has a different set of needs. Of course, heterosexist comments that he hears at work can still make him angry. At those times, he may attend meetings for his company's lesbian, gay, bisexual and transgender Employee Resource Group, so that he can process his experience with the right support network. Overall, though, Phillip does not feel that he can spend the rest of his life challenging discrimination and correcting behavior. He has found that it gets exhausting, though he knows that our culture still has a significant amount of necessary growth for equity to be realized.

In the workplace, it is necessary and valuable to actively reach out to those who are at Identity Synthesis, because they will have less need or desire to take advantage of the support networks that are in place. Additionally, they are a group that also supports the development of a corporate culture that is fully lesbian, gay, bisexual and transgender inclusive. Their experience can help overcome the same obstacles as individuals at the Identity Pride stage. Additionally, they may have close contacts in other circles in which it is helpful to build bridges. For example, perhaps they have become friendly with an executive whose child is in the same workplace childcare room as their own. Such relationships provide different avenues to build support from people who might not otherwise be paying attention to the lack of workplace equity.

Along with being knowledgeable about the individualized process of coming out, it is necessary to understand that the environment fostered at work can have a significant impact on the way in which a person goes through this process. Heterosexual executives and coworkers may not fully realize the immense energy that someone invests in both concealing an identity and in coming out. Truly comprehending the unique challenges of coming out as lesbian, gay, bisexual or transgender is essential to making the case for changing the corporate culture. Change requires a collaborative effort among allies *and* lesbian, gay, bisexual and transgender personnel to help others in the workplace understand the dynamics of these challenges and their impact on organizational development.

CHAPTER FOUR

Now That You're Out:
Responses to Coming Out in the Workplace

While individuals may start to come out during the stages of Identity Acceptance and Identity Pride, they inevitably encounter varying responses when they disclose that they are lesbian, gay, bisexual or transgender. Earlier we noted that people are far more likely to come out to family and friends than to workplace colleagues. The previous chapter analyzes the challenges involved in coming out to oneself and the weighing of the associated risks.

As a result of these challenges, coming out is a complicated and ongoing process for many people. This is a reality that heterosexuals may not be fully aware of, because they cannot fathom resistance, let alone anger, being directed at them for their own sexual orientation or identity. The associated risks can involve experiencing verbal attacks, physical assaults and employment discrimination. Lesbian, gay, bisexual and transgender individuals understandably weigh their desire and need to be out against the potentially negative consequences that they may encounter.

Vivian Cass's model, examined in the previous chapter, serves as an initial, valuable framework. The challenges identified during the stages of the Cass model exist because of the social expectation and enforcement of universal heterosexuality. These social norms have been created and reinforced by heterosexuals. In my view, this gives those who identify as heterosexual a responsibility to more closely examine the corrosive effect of this bias on people who are lesbian, gay, bisexual or transgender. Cass's model, while insightful and highly regarded, does not fully address the need for allies to focus on the environment created at work and how the atmosphere there can inhibit those who are lesbian, gay, bisexual or transgender from coming out.

FIGURE 4.1

Tips for Success: Responses to Coming Out

1. **Individuals have a lot to lose when coming out of the closet.** Coming out poses great personal risk for some individuals. Give thought to how to create a clearly supportive work environment.
2. **Individuals have a lot to gain when coming out of the closet.** Coming out allows a person to be honest about who he or she is and focus on workplace productivity rather than on hiding an important part of the self.
3. **Let people know that you can be part of their support network.** If people are looking for a support network, find ways to make it clear that you are willing to be a part of that network.
4. **Be a catalyst for creating a workplace culture that makes coming out easier.** Individuals are far more likely to come out to family and friends than workplace colleagues. Creating a more equitable work environment will encourage others to come out of the closet.

Some closeted individuals' questions and anxieties over coming out can be more easily alleviated if equal rights and a clear support network have been established at the job site. If no clear signs have been provided, there is a large range of responses that a lesbian, gay, bisexual, or transgender individual would reasonably anticipate. Some may fear the most negative responses possible, making coming out at work all the more challenging and even intimidating.

The Nelson Continuum

Professor and writer James B. Nelson has developed a continuum of religious responses to coming out: Rejecting Punitive, Rejecting Non-Punitive, Qualified Acceptance, and Full Acceptance.[57]

For *Allies at Work*, Nelson's analysis of a continuum has been adapted to the workplace. In contrast to the Cass model, this framework gives allies the responsibility for providing an opportunity to deconstruct the challenges and benefits of being openly lesbian, gay, bisexual or transgender.

The Nelson continuum offers concrete language to consider the responses and treatment individuals experience when they are openly lesbian, gay, bisexual or transgender. Each response is examined to better understand the challenges or benefits that accompany it. Nelson's approach is particularly useful for an allies program, because this framework can be utilized for examining how to move individuals, departments and entire corporations along the continuum. This chapter analyzes varied responses in the context of the workplace to demonstrate how attitudes can impact individual productivity as well as a company's efforts to serve as an employer-of-choice for lesbian, gay, bisexual and transgender employees and prospective employees.

Rejecting Punitive

Rejecting Punitive responses occur when someone is punished for his or her sexual orientation or gender identity/expression. The specific punishment for Rejecting Punitive typically involves physical or economic consequences for being lesbian, gay, bisexual or transgender. For example, in the United States military, currently the "Don't Ask, Don't Tell" policy requires firing someone found to be lesbian, gay, bisexual or transgender. As stated in previous chapters, no federal law protects workers from being fired because of their sexual orientation or gender identity/expression. Rejecting Punitive responses are also characterized by physical violence such as hate crimes committed against lesbian, gay, bisexual and transgender individuals.

In the workforce, manifestations of Rejecting Punitive behavior are far more likely to be economic than verbal or physical. However, physical Rejecting Punitive experiences impact the workplace, even when they occur outside of work. Obvious outcomes of physical violence may be work absences and higher health care premiums. Verbal attacks can also affect an employee's focus and productivity. For example, consider the experience of one employee of a major pharmaceutical company who was driving to work with a rainbow bumper sticker on her car. At a red light, a man in a pickup truck behind her got out and banged violently on her window, screaming derogatory comments and threatening her. While the incident did not result in bodily harm, when she arrived at her place of employment, the verbal attack and threats left her frightened and unable to work. The energy it takes to manage feelings after experiencing that kind of personal attack makes it nearly impossible to fully concentrate on work. However, the support that an employee finds at work can have a direct impact on how quickly she can recover and dedicate herself to her work. In some cases, though, the Rejecting Punitive response comes from the workplace itself. Rather than physical threats, lesbian, gay, bisexual and transgender individuals can lose their jobs.

Steve Stanton was a well-regarded city manager in Largo, Florida. Stanton received exemplary reviews and received a 9% raise for a salary of over $140,000 during his last year on the job. He held this job for 14 years. Stanton was transsexual, was planning to go through sex-reassignment surgery, and was already undergoing hormone therapy. He had disclosed this to a few close friends, family members and coworkers.

Stanton had planned to educate his coworkers about his transition, and he was waiting a few months to begin the wider and larger
process of workplace self-disclosure. However, one of the people
in whom he confided about undergoing hormone therapy leaked
the story to the *St. Petersburg Times*, and the paper considered his
personal information newsworthy. Stanton was outed. In less than
two weeks, Stanton was fired from his job.[58]

Rejecting Punitive treatment brings with it feelings such as depression and isolation. The isolation is often a form of self-protection.
Individuals who find themselves isolated may well fear coming out
due to the magnitude of the risk, whether their concerns are based in
reality or anxiety. In contrast, when persons identify as heterosexual,
they do not ever have to fear physical or economic punishment due
to their sexual orientation or gender identity/expression. Hiding
one's true identity as a lesbian, gay, bisexual or transgender person
sometimes provides protection from Rejecting Punitive behaviors.
However, this form of self-protection makes it difficult if not impossible to maintain a healthy sense of self. The impact of anticipating
or even experiencing a Rejecting Punitive work environment will
inevitably reduce workplace productivity. If a strong allies program
and support network are not in place, many individuals will prepare
themselves for the worst possible response.

Rejecting Non-Punitive

The next stage on the Nelson continuum, Rejecting Non-Punitive,
occurs when an individual is rejected for being lesbian, gay, bisexual
or transgender in a non-physical and non-economic manner. Rejecting Non-Punitive responses typically take the form of infliction
of emotional pain. It is likely to manifest in clear verbal statements
or situational cues that tell lesbian, gay, bisexual, or transgender
individuals that their identities and/or relationships are not just

socially unacceptable but also inferior. While Rejecting Non-Punitive behavior does not result in the economic and physical punishment associated with Rejecting Punitive, both stances evoke similar feelings in targeted lesbian, gay, bisexual or transgender individuals. When coping with the negative comments and cues typical of Rejecting Non-Punitive, individuals may feel less outright fear for their physical safety and economic security. However, the reality and consequences of isolation remain.

Rejecting Punitive Case Study   Estefan is 26 years old and was openly gay but is now partially back in the closet. He originally came out during his freshman year of college. The first person he told was a girl in his dorm with whom he had grown close. Her response was to hug him and share how happy she was that he felt safe first disclosing this to her. With the support of a close friend, Estefan soon came out to others. He was never the activist type, never a guy who wanted to lead the gay pride parade. In fact, he wasn't even the guy who attended the parade, though he supported the goals. He was never interested in being the center of attention.

Estefan majored in accounting and was brilliant with numbers. In college, he met his life partner, an artist. Upon graduation, they moved to a major East Coast city. Estefan's partner was out, and they would be seen together at various art events in the city. His partner was on the board of a major lesbian, gay, bisexual and transgender civil rights organization. Estefan was strongly supportive but had no desire to be an activist himself. He supported the goals of the organization and admired the community leaders. However, Estefan would only make donations anonymously, in keeping with his preference for privacy.

Estefan was not out at work. His supervisor occasionally sent out emails for political fundraisers or events. The emails never included personal notes advocating for the politician or the cause. Instead, Estefan's supervisor stressed the value of a strong community presence. However, most of the time these fundraisers were for elected officials or organizations that could only be described as anti-gay, lesbian, bisexual and transgender. Of course Estefan never attended these events. In fact, he attended few work-sponsored events, because he wanted to be with his partner and worried that they would not be welcome. Instead, he could go to his partner's events in the city without having to worry about being in the closet. He did have some concern about how missing work-related social activities might affect his future at the company, because being absent limited his networking opportunities.

The situation was challenging. Estefan felt that his supervisor was a good person. Estefan found the man to be kind and caring, always looking out for how his employees were feeling. He regularly complimented Estefan, even on occasion calling him brilliant. The only time Estefan felt particularly uncomfortable was when he received his boss's emails about politicians or groups that he found hurtful and disparaging. He knew his supervisor was not a hurtful individual, but Estefan also concluded that his supervisor might have a value system that rejected homosexuality.

Estefan's corporation posted a job opening for a manager in accounting. Estefan thought that he would be a strong candidate and knew that his major competition would be Sally, a talented coworker in his department. He and Sally had started working for the company at approximately the same time. Estefan had slightly better reviews, but Sally worked harder at being known. The management team knew the name of her husband, and she and her husband were at all of the corporate social events. Everyone liked her, everyone loved her husband, and Estefan knew he couldn't compete with her on a networking level. However, he was well aware that he had the skill set that made him the best fit for the position.

They both applied, and Sally received the promotion. After Estefan was turned down for the job, his boss told him that his time would come. Estefan carefully considered what had happened and concluded that the decisive factor was that Sally had made sure that her bosses knew her. Estefan knew that people always liked his partner, as he was absolutely charming. Estefan knew he was highly respected for the quality of his work and decided to bring his partner to the upcoming company family picnic. He first wanted to tell his boss, who had given him nothing but great reviews. Estefan knew that his boss regularly sent out conservative emails, but Estefan hoped that his boss's conservatism did not extend to sexual orientation.

Estefan began to convince himself that he had been misunderstanding his boss. He knew that being in the closet was taking up a lot of energy at work, consuming him at times, particularly now that he had been turned down for a promotion. Estefan stopped by his boss's office and after some small talk, he disclosed, "By the way, I don't think that you have ever met my partner. We worked out our schedule so that he can attend the company's Memorial Day family picnic."

Estefan saw a look of discomfort cross his boss's face, who then said, "Look, I couldn't care less if you are a gay, bisexual, reformed alcoholic, whatever. It doesn't matter to me. I value the fact that you are a great accountant for this company, and your hard work means a lot to us. Just remember that this is a family company. We are having a *family* picnic. The last thing I need is for people to boycott for moral objections. Remember, this is supposed to build morale and not become a political soapbox. It's not about showcasing alternative lifestyles. You're smart. You know what I mean."

What is valuable to note here is that this boss, while declaring that he was not prejudiced, revealed his bigotry under the banner of corporate loyalty. If Estefan were to defend his right to be treated equally, he would have to challenge his boss's beliefs and pit his own identity against what was being presented as the company's best interest. His choices were to either assert himself, a gesture that would be perceived to be at company's expense, or to protect his company at his own expense.

The feelings of alienation and isolation experienced during a Rejecting Non-Punitive reaction are comparable to those evoked by a Rejecting Punitive response. It is clear to people who are lesbian, gay, bisexual and transgender that they will not be accepted and are being regarded as morally deficient. While individuals will probably not get fired from their jobs in a Rejecting Non-Punitive environment, lesbian, gay, bisexual and transgender employees will reasonably fear that they will be passed over for promotions and receive bonuses than smaller they deserve, even though it is often difficult to prove any direct correlation. They know that their families will never be regarded as equal. Consequently, individuals may avoid coming out in this climate as a form of self-protection. As with a Rejecting Punitive response, this one has a corrosive effect on the individual and a subsequent impact on his job performance.

Rejecting Non Punitive Case Study   Brent Reinhard is a bright and charismatic 33-year-old who is quickly climbing the corporate ladder in a financial services Fortune 500 company. When he switched employers Brent began to wonder whether he had made the correct decision: "My first day at my current employer was right after Super Bowl Sunday in 2003. I was standing in my boss's office, and someone made a comment that they were at the Super Bowl party with gay guys, and they said all the gays talked about was the tight ends. He was relaying what he felt was a funny story. He was being negative about it. I was saying to myself, 'What the heck have I just gotten myself into?'"

Fortunately for Reinhard and his current employer, the episode was the exception rather than the rule. In fact, since arriving there, he has continued moving up the corporate ladder. The overall positive environment that the company has fostered for lesbian,

David M. Hall

gay, bisexual and transgender employees has allowed Reinhard to contextualize that experience and otherwise focus on being an effective employee.[59]

People who exhibit Rejecting Punitive behaviors might contend that they are doing nothing more than expressing views that they have every right to express. In many cases, they are expressing deeply held and perhaps even religiously based beliefs. While a free society cannot force people to be accepting of others' opinions or beliefs, the rejection of lesbian, gay, bisexual and transgender individuals stands in direct opposition to the goal of organizational effectiveness for a corporation. Biased attitudes undermine teamwork and cooperation by demanding, not mutual support and understanding, but absolute heterosexist conformity.

Qualified Acceptance

In the case of a Qualified Acceptance response, an individual often receives mixed signals about how others feel about lesbian, gay, bisexual and transgender people. A person finds Qualified Acceptance when there are some ways in which lesbian, gay, bisexual and transgender individuals are clearly provided with support, but also ways or times in which they are expected to conceal their identity. Within families, Qualified Acceptance can be evident when individuals are told that they can bring their partners along but not introduce them as such to grandparents, nieces or nephews. For example, a bisexual member of the family who is partnered with someone of the same sex might be cautioned by her sibling, "You can bring Jen to Mark's birthday party, but you need to introduce her to the children as your best friend, not as your partner."

In the workplace, Qualified Acceptance is expressed in a myriad of ways. A company might have an all-inclusive non-discrimination policy but no domestic partner benefits. Another may claim to offer domestic partner benefits which do not include family or bereavement leave. Qualified Acceptance may be exemplified not in the benefits package but in the corporate culture. For instance, a company that receives a high Diversity Index rating might also tell some employees to remove the rainbow stickers from their cubicles. As common as the experience of Qualified Acceptance may be for many lesbian, gay, and bisexual employees, this mixed reaction is often far more evident and explicit toward transgender employees.

Qualified Acceptance Case Study   Mary is currently receiving hormone therapy and planning to undergo sex reassignment surgery. She works in sales for a Fortune 200 company, and most of her work is conducted through travel and site visits. She is fortunate enough to work for a company that provides at least some benefits to cover the hormone therapy, though not the sex reassignment surgery. Without the job, she would never be able to afford the surgery. Within a year, Mary plans to begin presenting herself as Michael. Mary is aware of and self-conscious about the fact that people may stare at her during her transition and after she goes through sex reassignment surgery. She is worried that some staring will continue even after surgery because her body may not fully conform to the masculine model. For example, men and women's weight tends to be distributed differently, and, like most women, she carries more of it in her lower half.

Mary meets with her direct supervisor to talk about her plans, and he voices support for her. He reminds her of the benefits that the company has in place to support employees going through hormone therapy and urges Mary to take full advantage of those benefits.

"So what do you want me to call you when this whole thing is done?" he asks, appearing somewhat apprehensive.

"Eventually I will present myself as Michael."

Mary's boss sits in silence for a minute. He begins by speaking slowly, as if trying to carefully express himself: "Mary, I am not judging you. But let's be honest. This is not as American as apple pie. And we are in sales. At the end of the day, you and I are judged based on what we produce. What happens when clients meet a guy named Michael whom they know is not a real man?"

"Look, go through the therapy. Even get the surgery if you want. But can't you pick a name that doesn't let on? How about Jean? Pat? Chris? Sam? There are plenty of better choices out there. Just think about it. Don't forget why you and I are here. It is to make money. I am glad for you that you are doing what you need to do, but don't let it hurt our bottom line. We are all here to do what's best for the company. And I know that you don't want to do anything that would hurt our corporation. Right?"

Under Qualified Acceptance, lesbian, gay, bisexual and transgender workers experience feelings during this stage that are similar to feelings during the experiences of Rejecting Punitive and Rejecting Non-Punitive. A company can have many of the right policies in place, but the corporate culture may not provide an atmosphere of acceptance for someone who is lesbian, gay, bisexual or transgender. Individuals may not fear losing their jobs or being physically hurt. Yet they daily encounter situations in which they know that their coworkers see them as less than equal, and this judgment will emerge without mainstream colleagues realizing how hurtful or insensitive they are being. When they meet ignorance, they must constantly decide if they want to intervene and educate someone or if they want to avoid conflict and go on their way. Every corporation wants its employees to direct their energy to their workplace responsibilities.

Full Acceptance

Full Acceptance is the response lesbian, gay, bisexual and transgender individuals experience when treated with equity. This does not mean that heterosexism does not assert itself at times. It certainly may, and it may even be expressed by an individual who is working at being supportive and an ally. In these instances, the heterosexism may be the easiest to address and correct. Lesbian, gay and bisexual employees may find that they are more likely to experience Full Acceptance than their transgender coworkers do. This is reflected in a variety of ways. First, there is, in general society and the popular media, more exposure to lesbian, gay and bisexual individuals than to transgender people. Second, corporate policies further reflect this. Most large companies prohibit discrimination based on sexual orientation, but less than 50% offer the same protection based on gender identity.[60]

Overall, those who express Full Acceptance are the ideal workplace allies. Some allies even demonstrate a commitment to working to change the corporate culture. Allies sometimes join their Employee Resource Group. Motivations of those who exhibit Full Acceptance may include having someone in their family, work or friendship circles who is lesbian, gay, bisexual or transgender, or they may have other altruistic motivations. In a later chapter, we will more closely examine allies' motivations and some strategies for inspiring allies to take on leadership roles.

Full Acceptance Case Study   Takita is a mid-level manager in the human resources diversity office of her Fortune 100 Company. She was recruited from her company's primary competitor. When she arrived at her new workplace, she placed a picture on her desk showing herself with her female partner on a cruise ship. Her direct supervisor came in to welcome her and saw the picture. Previously, she had no idea what Takita's sexual orientation was, because Takita had not come out during the job interview. The supervisor saw the picture and began talking with Takita about her partner. Then she said, "Well, how about you and your partner have dinner with my husband and me this weekend to welcome you to our great city?"

Takita accepted the invitation, and she and her partner had a great evening with them.

Takita joined and quickly became an officer in her company's lesbian, gay, bisexual and transgender Employee Resource Group. Her heterosexual supervisor also joined the group. They and others collaborated on developing new programs for diversity training, raising awareness during Pride month, and making the company policies more lesbian, gay, bisexual and transgender-friendly. Takita's boss placed a rainbow flag sticker on her door and occasionally sent out emails to the department featuring notable lesbian, gay, bisexual and transgender people in history.

Takita has found strong support in her new workplace. She sends her children to the company daycare, which has a collection of diverse children's books, including some that depict same-sex parents. She and her partner attend company events, and she rarely feels treated differently from her heterosexual colleagues.

While Full Acceptance can involve playing a leadership role or acting as a high profile ally, a person can also demonstrate that he is an ally through simple conversation. For example, when speaking with a supervisor he trusted, Reinhard, a financial services employee, said, "I just had this horrible fight with Jim this morning."

His supervisor responded, smiling, "Are you actually going to tell me that he is your boyfriend?" Her words and manner let him know that she had been waiting for an opportunity to show she was supportive.

Reinhard confirmed that he was and found that not only was she fully accepting, but that his workplace was also. "So I don't know why I worried about coming out," he said. He then quickly added that he does know why and revealed a perspective that every ally needs to understand: "I waited for people to give me signs before I told them."[61]

Part of Full Acceptance that allies need to understand is that they have to provide clear signs that they are, in fact, allies and not adversaries. No matter how strong one's relationship may be with coworkers, they will not know how one feels about lesbian, gay, bisexual and transgender individuals unless it is made clear.

Janet Smith, a senior executive at Citigroup, says that she considered herself supportive of her colleagues and cared about fairness in the workplace, but she came to realize that she hadn't communicated her views to her coworkers: "I'm a straight ally, which I feel very, very strongly about, but I didn't realize until I went through an experience with a work colleague as she was outed at work—and she didn't necessarily want to be outed at work. I saw her pain, and I realized how important it is to also be out as an ally. If all you do is know you're out [as an ally], but you don't actually take affirmative steps to share how you feel at work, then you're not helping. You're part of the problem."[62]

Full Acceptance is the first and only place on the Nelson continuum where someone who is lesbian, gay, bisexual or transgender begins to have consistent positive experiences and feelings when they come out of the closet. A company that makes Full Acceptance its policy and practice allows employees to excel. They can use a minimal amount of energy protecting themselves from discrimination.

Knowing that one's supervisors and company are supportive and accepting builds good will and company loyalty. If another company attempts to hire away a talented employee who enjoys Full Acceptance at her workplace, she may hesitate to leave her employer. Even when she can earn more money elsewhere, she may be reluctant to give other prospects much consideration, because the acceptance and freedom that she experiences at work is something that means a great deal to her and cannot be taken for granted. Full Acceptance maximizes company loyalty and workplace productivity.

Virtually every workplace is at a different point on the Nelson continuum, depending on the department and environment. For example, a company that has made a dedicated effort to create an LGBT-inclusive workplace could have people in some departments—particularly diversity or human resources—who rate their company at Full Acceptance. However, employees in other departments may consider their company to be Rejecting Punitive. The Nelson continuum provides each corporation with a means to analyze their corporate culture and develop ways to improve. The demands may vary depending on department and geographic location. For example, Chris Eagan, who works for a Fortune 500 pharmaceutical company, explains that she feels accepted but would not expect the same reaction across her company: "I don't feel at my site—and I will say at my site—that there are any issues. But I would feel differently if I worked at a different site. My site had a little bit of a different culture than the rest of the company, because we were acquired. I have talked to people who have been at home office and corporate. There are not a lot of out people."[63]

Where is your company on this continuum? Is that placement acceptable? Does your company need to move further along the continuum? If your company needs to progress further, allies have a responsibility and a critical role to play in transforming the corporate culture.

How Do We Use the Continuum?

We live in a society in which it is unrealistic to expect everyone to be fully accepting of homosexuality. Many people have a value system that does not have room for Full Acceptance or even Qualified Acceptance, though these individuals may be relatively polite in public about how they express their lack of acceptance. This creates significant workplace challenges. Everyone, including lesbian, gay, bisexual or transgender people, wants to work in environments in which they experience Full Acceptance. At the same time, some managers and coworkers will assert the right to hold and express unsupportive or even narrow-minded views, including personal opinions about morality.

This creates significant challenges for people committed to diversity and inclusion. People who are passionate about an issue want others to agree with them. However, a goal in education, particularly in diversity education, is to challenge people to grow in relationship to themselves. As a result, if we expect everyone to reach the level of Full Acceptance after a brief conversation or short diversity program, we are likely to experience disappointment, continued frustration and eventual burn out. The obstacles to Full Acceptance are deeply ingrained for many.

Some may have a value system that prohibits them from reaching Full Acceptance. Patience is required to ensure that people have the opportunity to explore these issues in relationship to their own value system. Diversity programs may need to encourage people to challenge themselves to move along this continuum in a way that works best for them. If we attempt to force others to adopt our views, they are likely to shut down in order to protect their deeply held beliefs.

For example, some employees may belong to a group that actively opposes homosexuality. It is highly unlikely that they will become fully accepting of lesbian, gay, bisexual and transgender individuals in the near future, if ever. However, perhaps an effective allies program could move them from Rejecting Punitive to Rejecting Non-Punitive. This may be far removed from where we need people to be for an equitable workplace or, indeed, a world that respects our basic humanity. Yet it is unquestionably preferable—and less costly to companies and individuals—to reduce worksite expressions of hatred, bullying behavior and harassment.

Those who are Rejecting Non-Punitive can be taught that their attitude is not in the company's best interest and conflicts with the company's determination to foster a highly motivated and dedicated workforce. By such methods, we can attempt to move them to Qualified Acceptance, if for no other reason than for the good of the company. Similarly, those who are at Qualified Acceptance and learn about bias and heterosexual privilege can move toward Full Acceptance. Staff diversity and AIDS education trainings can help reduce bias by addressing stereotypes and correcting commonly held misinformation. The policies of many Fortune 500 companies reflect Full Acceptance, but the corporate culture—in the office or the warehouse—reflects something less. It is in the best economic interest of corporations to have not only policies but also onsite practices and management commitment to support and reflect Full Acceptance.

Moving companies' policies and workplace culture along this continuum should be an ongoing goal. Policies are much easier to change than culture. That is why corporations that truly value equity go beyond getting a perfect rating on an LGBT diversity index. They work to change the corporate culture, so that they can be employers-of-choice. "At the end of the day," says Selisse Berry, executive director of Out & Equal, "workplace equality is not just about the policies companies put in place. Workplace equality is about creating a culture of inclusiveness that encourages employees to bring their whole selves to work."

Marla Schlenoff, who works at Goldman Sachs's corporate headquarters in the Office of Global Leadership and Diversity, says that the company's commitment to lesbian, gay, bisexual and transgender diversity—and to all strands of diversity—helps her firm attract applicants and encourages employee loyalty. She adds that this is true for other Wall Street firms, and that they keep an eye on their business competitors: "We often benchmark ourselves against other financial services firms."

Marla has noticed that the younger talent pool, made up of many recent college graduates, tends to be more open-minded about lesbian, gay, bisexual and transgender issues. They are more likely to be at ease about being out in the workplace and to expect their employers to have domestic partner benefits and Employee Resource Groups in place. "I think it's really prudent for us to understand where people are coming from, what desires they have, in order for us to be a firm of choice. And we want people not only to come through recruiting, but then to retain them as well. We need to be on the pulse of what's going on and what people want."[64]

Some heterosexual employees who are at Full Acceptance need to be motivated to lead. They are the allies who work for fundamental changes in the corporate culture. Their advocacy for their coworkers can play a powerful role in helping move others along the continuum. To meet corporate diversity goals, allies and their lesbian, gay, bisexual and transgender colleagues must work collectively to move individuals toward more progressive stages of the Nelson continuum. By doing so, they are embarking on a continuous journey in moving toward workplace equity.

CHAPTER FIVE

From the Lavender Scare to Today's Workplace Equality: A Brief History

"In the opinion of this subcommittee homosexuals and other sex perverts are not proper persons to be employed in Government for two reasons; first, they are generally unsuitable, and second, they constitute security risks."

Subcommittee Report

United States Senate, 1950 [65]

"We offer fair and equal policies for LGBT employees, provide great services and customized financial advice to our diverse customers, and our team members are actively involved in LGBT non-profit organizations and community programs."

Julie White,

Director of Human Resources

Wells Fargo & Co., 2008 [66]

Restructuring workplace policies and practices in order to produce a more open and equitable work climate involves far more than written guidelines and their enforcement. In fact, it requires acknowledging the bias and injustice that exist and working to educate people and uphold job site standards of behavior, so that the bigotry that permeates much of our society is limited or harmless in the workplace. To understand today's issues in context, it is important to be aware of the history of homophobia and heterosexism. This chapter offers a brief, introductory history of discrimination against lesbian, gay, bisexual and transgender Americans.

David M. Hall

Following our historical review, Chapter Six analyzes the workplace environment that makes a company an employer-of-choice for lesbian, gay, bisexual and transgender workers. We look at bias and attitudes that interfere with a company's ability or willingness to move toward workplace inclusion.

In Chapter Two we discussed the 5 P's, starting with Protection. Using Protection, we can examine how well workplace policies reflect not only our humanity and our vision of the world in which we want to live, but also the principles of organizational development that lead to becoming an employer-of-choice.

The Legacy of Discrimination

The bias experienced by lesbian, gay, bisexual and transgender employees is not a modern construction but is anchored in a painful history of discriminatory laws. In colonial times, a man caught having sex with another man had committed an offense punishable by death.[67] The word "homosexual" was not coined until the 19th century, and it was only during the past hundred years that public policy deemed homosexuality to be an identity and not just a behavior.

During World War II, military discrimination against gay men became official policy when males were screened with the question, "Do you like girls?" Additionally, the military expelled gay men based on their "feminine bodily characteristics" and "effeminacy in dress or manner."[68] The United States military began to exclude lesbians in 1944. It is considered likely that there were a sizable number of lesbians serving our nation in the Women's Army Corps, because in that era married women were not permitted to enlist and pregnant women were automatically discharged. However, the overwhelming majority of personnel who were discharged were either gay men or men deemed to be gay.[69]

FIGURE 5.1

Tips for Success: The Legacy of Discrimination

1. **There is a long history of legal discrimination based on sexual orientation and gender identity**. We have evolved significantly from an era when it was federal policy to fire government employees based on their sexual orientation.

2. **The legacy of that discrimination still exists.** While most of the federal government does not maintain such discriminatory policies, they still exist in the U.S. military and in many work environments.

3. **Lesbian, gay, bisexual and transgender individuals still face laws that fail to treat them equally.**

4. **Changing corporate culture requires dedicated work.** Such change will not occur without effort. Creating change for the sake of organizational development requires planning, commitment and thoughtful action.

Sadly, military service was not the only area of discriminatory practices for the United States government. The denigration of lesbian, gay, bisexual and transgender individuals—which still permeates the U.S. military—became a rapidly spreading witch-hunt throughout the federal government during the 1950s. Destroying thousands of lives each year, a "gay panic" spread across the federal and state governments, perpetuating the unsubstantiated notion that employing gay people weakens American democracy.

In 1950, a United States Senate subcommittee issued a report titled "Employment of Homosexuals and Other Sex Perverts in Government." The report was a blistering and hysterical attack on lesbian, gay, bisexual and transgender individuals working for the federal government. The report began by citing homosexuality's "immorality" and violation of "normal standards of social behavior," often using the word "pervert" as synonymous and interchangeable with homosexual. Much of the report warned of the supposed certainty of homosexual recruitment: "These perverts will frequently attempt to entice normal individuals to engage in perverted practices.... [If] a homosexual attains a position in Government where he can influence the hiring of personnel, it is almost inevitable that he will attempt to place other homosexuals in government jobs."[70]

The Senate report concluded that "one homosexual can pollute an entire Government office" and cited the "lack of emotional stability" and a homosexual's "weakness of ... moral fiber" as rationales for discriminatory policies.[71] Furthermore, the report contended that firing lesbian, gay, bisexual and transgender individuals was insufficient in its severity. While the subcommittee members complained that too many homosexuals were still employed by the federal government, they also criticized the fact that those who were fired were too often dismissed "in as quiet a manner as possible and circumvented the established rules with respect to the removal or dismissal of unsuitable personnel for Government positions."[72] Indeed, the United States Senate was seemingly calling for a 20th century Scarlet Letter and intending not just to personally but also publicly destroy lives through bigotry under the guise of protecting national security.

One year after the subcommittee's report, the book *Washington Confidential* included the assertion that "there are at least 6,000 homosexuals on the government payroll."[73] This book was followed by the Lavender Scare, a witch-hunt similar to the anti-communist Red Scare but targeting gay men and, to a lesser degree, lesbians and cross-dressers.[74] United States Senator Kenneth Wherry, a member of the Republican leadership at the time, was committed to removing all homosexuals from all positions in the federal government.[75] Soon his agenda would become official policy.

In 1953, President Eisenhower signed Executive Order 10450, which required the firing of homosexuals from federal employment. The order contained the following language identifying those who should be fired or denied employment: "Any criminal, infamous, dishonest, immoral, or notoriously disgraceful conduct, habitual use of intoxicants to excess, drug addiction, sexual perversion." During the early Cold War, it is estimated that about 5,000 gay men and lesbians lost their jobs.[76]

Persecution pervaded government policies to the point that the FBI raided gay bars and other gathering places, and postal inspectors subscribed to gay pen pal clubs in an effort to trace the other subscribers. Beginning in the 1950s, a Florida committee spent nine years investigating communists, civil rights leaders and gay men and lesbians working in academia and public education. Teachers and professors lost their jobs, and education majors dropped out of college—certain that they would be persecuted once they entered public service. In 1957, even the American Civil Liberties Union abandoned gays and lesbians by adopting a policy that supported upholding state sodomy laws.[77]

While (outside of the military) there is currently no federal policy to fire lesbian, gay, bisexual and transgender individuals, doing so remains perfectly legal in much of the private sector. In his 2003 dissent in the case of *Lawrence v. Texas*, the case which legalized private, consensual acts of sodomy, U.S. Supreme Court Justice Antonin Scalia passionately argued that such discrimination should remain legal: "Many Americans do not want persons who openly engage in homosexual conduct as partners in their business, as scoutmasters for their children, as teachers in their children's schools, or as boarders in their home. They view this as protecting themselves and their families from a lifestyle that they believe to be immoral and destructive."[78]

David M. Hall

States Today Expanding Same-Sex Couples' Rights

Across the country, companies are developing more accepting workplace environments at the same time that a number of states are reviewing or expanding familial rights for same-sex couples. Examining recent political history helps deepen understanding of the contemporary atmosphere of workplace inclusion.

A national debate over marriage equality, which is the updated term for same-sex marriage, began in 1993 when the Hawaii Supreme Court ruled that a prohibition against same-sex marriage violated Hawaii's constitution without demonstrating a compelling state interest. In 1996, a Hawaiian trial court ruled that no compelling state interest could be demonstrated and that the prohibition against marriage equality was unconstitutional. Before the appeal reached the Hawaii Supreme Court, voters in the state amended their state constitution to prohibit same-sex couples from marrying. Also in 1996, the Alaska Superior Court ruled in favor of same-sex couples, and voters amended their state constitution to ban marriage equality two years later.[79]

As a result of the state lawsuits and national dialogue, the U.S. Congress passed a federal law defining marriage as between a man and a woman. In 1996, President Clinton signed into law the Defense of Marriage Act.[80]

On December 20, 1999, the Supreme Court of Vermont ruled that same-sex couples deserve the same legal protections as married, heterosexual couples. The court ruled that the Common Benefits Clause of the Vermont Constitution protects same-sex couples: "We hold that the State is constitutionally required to extend to same-sex couples the common benefits and protections that flow from marriage under Vermont law." The court allowed the state legislature to decide whether to extend the right of marriage or domestic partner benefits to same-sex couples in Vermont.[81] Howard Dean, then Governor of Vermont, signed a bill making Vermont the first state in the country to authorize civil unions for same-sex couples.[82] This legislation afforded same-sex couples in Vermont the same state rights and privileges of marriage, though federal benefits remained out of reach. Other states have also expanded the rights of same-sex couples through various forms of domestic partner relationship recognition.

On November 18, 2003, the Massachusetts Supreme Judicial Court ruled that the Commonwealth of Massachusetts must also allow the marriage of same-sex couples. On May 17, 2004, same-sex couples were legally married for the first time in American history.[83] Swept up in this movement for equity, various municipalities outside of Massachusetts offered marriage licenses despite state laws prohibiting same-sex marriages: San Francisco, California, on February 12, 2004; Sandoval County, New Mexico on February 20, 2004; New Paltz, New York, on February 27, 2004; Multnomah County, Oregon, on March 3, 2004; and Asbury Park, New Jersey, on March 8, 2004.[84] A national dialogue on marriage ensued.

Rhetoric in opposition to marriage equality escalated following the Massachusetts decision: "I would argue that the future of our country hangs in the balance because the future of marriage hangs in the balance," declared Pennsylvania Senator Rick Santorum, the third-ranking Republican in the United States Senate.[85] At the federal level, a proposed constitutional amendment to outlaw marriage equality was introduced, reading:

SECTION 1. This article may be cited as the 'Marriage Protection Amendment'.
SECTION 2. Marriage in the United States shall consist only of the union of a man and a woman. Neither this Constitution nor

the constitution of any State, shall be construed to require that marriage or the legal incidents thereof be conferred upon any union other than the union of a man and a woman.[86]

The amendment passed neither the House of Representatives nor the Senate.

However, a variety of state ballot initiatives were introduced to ban marriage equality through state constitutional amendments. On Election Day 2004, the loss was overwhelming for lesbian, gay, bisexual and transgender rights groups. That day, the closest vote on a ballot initiative took place in Oregon, where organizations spent roughly the same amount of money for and against the measure. This was the first time that citizens in Oregon had voted on the issue of same-sex marriage language being added to their state constitution. Still, opposition to marriage equality prevailed by 57 to 43%. In state elections across the nation, 21 million people voted on the issue of marriage equality, and 14 million of them voted against it.[87]

Since then, a number of states have passed domestic partner benefits laws, and in 2006, voters in Arizona were the first in the nation to reject a statewide constitutional amendment that banned marriage equality, although the state still does not permit such marriages. In May 2008, the California Supreme Court ruled that the state was discriminating by banning same-sex marriages. Governor Arnold Schwarzenegger, who had previously vetoed legislation permitting marriage equality, said that the California Supreme Court decision should be respected and upheld. A subsequent ballot initiative, Proposition 8, to amend the California state constitution with the declaration that only marriage between a man and a woman would be valid or recognized, was narrowly passed in November 2008. The following year, a California State Supreme Court ruling upheld Proposition 8. At the time of this writing, pending legal challenges to the initiative make its long-term effect unclear.

If gender identity or sexual orientation is treated or regarded as inferior and unequal in the public domain, the cultural norm outside of a company inhibits true workplace equity even when an institution makes a sincere and dedicated effort for equity and inclusion. American family law upholds a relationship hierarchy and gives more power to heterosexuals, at the expense of people who are not. These laws often reflect the underlying values of a vociferous, conservative minority in American society. Creating true workplace equity must take cultural norms into consideration. Too often, there is a failure to recognize the broader experience of discrimination and its impact on individuals.

Because of the historical legacy of homophobia and heterosexism, efforts to create workplace equity for lesbian, gay, bisexual and transgender individuals in American companies amount to more than just advocating for change. We need to challenge the long and painful American legal practice of bigotry and oppression. It is within this context that remarkable strides are being made to create a more inclusive workforce. The next chapter identifies concrete policies and begins to explore the challenging dynamic of transforming the corporate culture.

CHAPTER SIX

Tools to Measure Corporate Effectiveness on Equality Issues

Following the example of anti-apartheid activists who put pressure on companies doing business with South Africa, in 1992 a small group of activists developed a set of Equality Principles, to help guide companies in creating equitable workplaces for gay and lesbian employees. These principles were used to develop a measurement tool, originally known as the Gay Lesbian Value Index, to hold corporations accountable for their polices and practices.

Since that time, several tools have been developed to measure corporate effectiveness on lesbian, gay, bisexual and transgender issues in the workplace. Stonewall UK developed the Workplace Equality Index, which measures corporate policies and practices in the United Kingdom. The International Gay and Lesbian Chamber of Commerce has developed the International Business Equality Index, which measures how companies around the world are performing on issues related to the lesbian, gay, bisexual and transgender community. Two of the better-known measures of corporate effectiveness on equality issues are Out & Equal's Steps to an Out & Equal Workplace and the Human Rights Campaign's Corporate Equality Index.

Out & Equal Workplace Advocates has identified specific steps toward creating an equitable work environment. These steps provide an educational tool that companies can use to identify areas of strength and focus on areas for growth in building an inclusive corporate environment for lesbian, gay, bisexual and transgender employees and customers. The best practices have evolved over time and now include a series of concrete steps that organizations can take to achieve workplace equality. Several steps are focused on company policies. However, Out & Equal's steps provide guidance in such areas as corporate climate, talent development and community involvement.

Steps to an Out & Equal Workplace

Policies and benefits
- Include sexual orientation in global non-discrimination and anti-harassment policies
- Include gender identity and expression in global non-discrimination and anti-harassment policies
- Recognize same-sex couples and their families with equal access to all company benefits
- Ensure that global health coverage includes complete health benefits for transgender employees

Talent management and professional development
- Establish and support LGBT Employee Resource Groups
- Recruit, hire, and offer mentoring to LGBT employees through tools such as **Out & Equal's LGBTCareerLink.com**
- Provide leadership development experiences specifically for LGBT employees
- Track recruitment and career development metrics for LGBT employees who choose to self identify

Workplace climate
- Provide diversity training with specific reference to LGBT issues—such as **Out & Equal's Building Bridges Training**—for all employees

- Use anonymous climate surveys to measure effectiveness of LGBT diversity policies and programs
- Include LGBT diversity objectives in management performance goals
- Communicate routinely to all employees about how the organization supports its LGBT workforce

Commitment to the community

- Support nonprofit groups working for LGBT equality
- Sponsor and encourage visible participation in LGBT cultural events
- Include LGBT images in marketing and advertising strategies
- Include LGBT-owned businesses in supplier diversity program objectives

Corporate responsibility & advocacy

- Be a visible role model for LGBT workplace equality in the community
- Support public policy efforts that protect LGBT workplace equality
- Speak out and counter attempts that would limit or restrict the rights of LGBT employees
- Share best practices that advance LGBT workplace equality by participating in the **Out & Equal Workplace Summit!**[88]

There is no fixed approach to implementing the Steps to an Out & Equal Workplace. The steps need not be achieved in the order suggested by the list. Many companies have found it useful to make their first objective the inclusion of sexual orientation in their nondiscrimination and anti-harassment policies. Every workplace is different and can best determine its own course of action to address the specific needs of the organization. For example, some

David M. Hall

companies have first revised their nondiscrimination policies to include sexual orientation and then later added similar provisions for gender identity. However, other companies have added both provisions to their policies in a single step.

Marcelo Roman, an IBM executive who leads the company's global learning delivery outsourcing services, recommends taking a flexible approach to creating an inclusive workplace, and shares his view that the process is not strictly linear. "You have a number of different entry points," he explains. "For example, Out & Equal has identified what we call Steps to an Out & Equal Workplace, but in my opinion, they're not in any one particular order. They are in a circle, and you can enter the circle at any point depending on where you are in your company. But then you can navigate through the circle and be able to connect to all the other points."

The goal of mechanisms like the Steps to an Out & Equal Workplace or the Corporate Equality Index is to hold companies accountable for how equitably they treat their lesbian, gay, bisexual and transgender employees. Corporations are rated with a percentage score based on their responses to the survey. The Human Rights Campaign annually surveys Fortune 500 companies and ranks them through the Corporate Equality Index. While some corporations choose not to complete the survey, many not only complete the survey but also consider their scores part of their plans to realize a competitive advantage with employees and consumers.

Such companies tend to see the value of their scores in terms of a broad sense of good workplace practices and inclusive policies to build consumer confidence. The ways in which a company values the impact on consumers will often depend on whether lesbian, gay, bisexual and transgender individuals consume their products. However, though Fortune 500 defense contractor companies are not selling to a lesbian, gay, bisexual and transgender market, they still want to hire from across the spectrum to bring together the most talented workforce possible. In contrast, credit card companies' policies reflect their market position. They want to be not only an employer-of-choice but also a beneficiary of lesbian, gay, bisexual and transgender disposable income.

Many corporate executives want their companies to be publicly singled out for praise for obtaining a perfect rating on a lesbian, gay, bisexual and transgener diversity scorecard. As summed up by Jennifer Jonach, director of human resources at Dupont, "We share the belief that an environment of equality and inclusiveness is essential so that employees may contribute to their fullest."[89] Hayward Bell, chief diversity officer for Raytheon, expressed a similar view, explaining, "Our commitment to diversity and inclusion is our undeniable pathway to success for individuals and the company——for everyone, every day and everywhere."[90]

Brian Schipper, senior vice president for human resources at Cisco Systems, took the argument a step further and recognized the impact of inclusive policies on a collaborative and creative work environment. "At Cisco, valuing all our employees isn't just the right thing to do, we know that it makes good business sense. Diverse teams foster a creative, innovative workforce, enabling collaboration across the company, to deliver products and services for our customers."[91]

Beyond simply serving as employers-of-choice for greater workplace productivity, some companies want their consumers to be well aware of their support for lesbian, gay, bisexual and transgender individuals. Ron Gillum, vice president at General Motors, noted the company's commitment to demonstrating support for lesbian, gay, bisexual and transgender consumers of automobiles: "showing GLBT customers that we support the community and appreciate their business."[92]

Sandy Price, senior vice president of human resources for SprintNextel Corporation, combines the value of a diverse workforce with its impact in reaching consumers: "At Sprint, diversity is an essential part of the way we do business. We're working hard to create an inclusive workplace that ensures all voices and points of view are valued and respected. This, in turn, allows us to reach a broader base of customers with products and services that truly add value to their lives."[93]

Lesbian, gay, bisexual and transgender diversity surveys have proven to be invaluable resources for getting employers to focus on equitable workplace treatment of lesbian, gay, bisexual and transgender individuals. These mechanisms provide corporations with specific criteria to become an employer-of-choice. Furthermore, these are important tools for helping employees choose where they will work.

These measurement tools examine the best practices for an inclusive work environment and evaluate companies based on their nondiscrimination policies and employee and family benefits. Non-discrimination policies include sexual orientation and gender identity protections, including consideration of how employees express their gender.[94]

Non-discrimination policies cover not just job protection but also workplace harassment and bullying. James Halleman, a steel manufacturing worker from Pennsylvania, shared his story of the harassment he experienced when transitioning: "I was given pretty much some of the heaviest labor that they had available on a daily basis. I had coworkers walk off the line, and I was left there by myself. Help came, but it was slow in coming. Just basically being around that environment—my significant other was afraid that one day I would end up in the furnace. So it did have its very scary moments."[95]

Without the passage of ENDA, the Employment Non-Discrimination Act, there are no federal protections from discrimination based on sexual orientation or gender identity/expression. James Halleman found that his state, the Commonwealth of Pennsylvania, also lacked such workplace protections. As a result, he could only look to his employer for help, and hope that human decency would prevail, since the law deemed him unworthy of equal protection. Indeed, many companies have filled this legal gap. Over the years, there has been a steady increase in companies including sexual orientation and gender identity in their non-discrimination policies.

Most effectiveness measures examine areas including domestic partner benefits, domestic partner affidavits and transgender health benefits.[96] The absence of domestic partner benefits creates demands on the same-sex families that heterosexual families rarely consider or could even imagine. As one closeted school teacher explained, "Neither my partner nor I receive domestic partner benefits. We are going to have a baby in a few months through a surrogate. One of us wants to stay home full-time. However, it is difficult enough to live on one income, and we cannot do it if we also have to pay for health care."[97] As a result, they both need to work even though they feel that this arrangement is not in the best interest of their family.

Heterosexuals who are not close to someone who is lesbian, gay, bisexual or transgender may not give any thought to this burden or to the challenges that this creates for a company. Such a fundamental lack of fairness in workplace policies has an impact on family life. Indeed, a simple question to ask heterosexual employees would be, "Given the choice, would you work for a company that provides family benefits or does not provide family benefits?" As more companies are providing domestic partner benefits, it is becoming increasingly difficult for any company that denies these benefits to become an employer-of-choice for lesbian, gay, bisexual and transgender individuals. This places companies that deny benefits at a competitive disadvantage.

Workplace adoption of domestic partner benefits—a critical workplace inclusion for lesbian, gay, bisexual and transgender employees—often requires hard work and advocacy. Partnering with allies can be critical in bringing about such policy changes, particularly at companies in which only a small number of people disclose at work that they are lesbian, gay, bisexual or transgender.

According to Louise Young, a senior software engineer at Raytheon and a founder of the company's Employee Resource Group, "Allies play a key role in our being able to achieve GLBT equality in the workplace. It's an indispensable role. Allies are really somewhat the catalyst for change within our corporations. Very often our allies are in decision-making positions. And so as we LGBT workplace advocates try to implement change, raise the bar and increase best practices at our companies, we look to our allies to help us."[98]

Chris Eagan, an employee at a Fortune 500 pharmaceutical company, explained the role that allies played in the adoption of domestic partner benefits at her workplace: "I would have to think that there had to be some allies at work behind the scenes that got domestic partner benefits to pass. I've asked from the day I started there, and it finally passed. There had to be allies to help push that through. They didn't see a lot of out people."[99]

It is encouraging that companies like Eagan's are moving in the direction of equal policies, though there are many facets to domestic partner benefits that may not be immediately apparent to all employers. It is important to stress that domestic partner benefits are not limited to health care benefits but should also include family and medical leave, bereavement leave, company transfers and other benefits that are extended to married heterosexual employees.

When initially launched, many corporate effectiveness tools did not include gender identity and transgender topics. However, in the last several years most organizations have added gender identity and transgender topics into their metrics. The process of gender transitioning, even without including sex-reassignment surgery, is expensive. The Corporate Equality Index identifies comprehensive transgender health coverage as including mental health counseling, hormone therapy, medical visits, surgical procedures and short-term medical leave.[100] For many companies, the transgender-related benefits package is their weakest area of coverage.

Across the country, hundreds of corporations have instituted policy and benefits changes that contribute to high ratings on LGBT equality measurement tools. However, when I speak at company events, meetings or diversity trainings, I ask participants to give their company a grade based on their own, personal LGBT equality index. In fact, I place signs around the room and have people stand by the grade that they would give their company. I have yet to find anyone who gives his or her workplace a grade as high as the company's ranking on an external measurement device. The day-to-day experience of a job or a worksite's atmosphere may be quite different from measurable factors such as board and management policies or company benefits programs. Addressing workplace climate is complex and involves many players at different levels within the corporate structure.

Personal relationships are key to establishing a positive and productive work environment. Consequently, formal measurement tools have their limitations. Dr. Richard Friend, a diversity and leadership consultant, identifies one of the biggest challenges as "the tendency to focus on systems and processes—the bricks and mortar of culture, rather than the experience of the culture which occurs inside the walls. We devote lots of energy into Employee Resource Groups and money into getting on the Corporate Equality Index. They might even join the National Gay and Lesbian Chamber of Commerce. All of which are important, but often the focus is more about the report card and the measure, rather than also attending to the relationships people are building with their supervisors, peers and customers. People may join an organization because of the bricks and mortar, but they leave or stay due to the relationships. It is the latter that is much harder to quantify and measure." [101]

As has been demonstrated throughout this book, we live in a society that does not treat lesbian, gay, bisexual and transgender individuals and their families equally. This discrepancy is felt both at work and in the larger community. As a result, even companies that receive a perfect rating from an LGBT equality effectiveness tool should still be taking steps to create a more equitable work environment, as there is often pervasive individual and institutional resistance, or even hostility, to equality. This raises the challenge of where and how training can be provided in order to transform corporate culture.

Richard Friend explains that the message of inclusion is understood differently in various facets of the company: "There's a disconnect. I think that the challenge happens at a couple of different levels. There is a squeeze in the middle. Middle managers are being urged to do more with less. They have to get more done with fewer resources. Senior executives are pushing from the top."[102] While it is essential that high-ranking executives better understand the need for lesbian, gay, bisexual and transgender inclusion and set performance standards, true inclusion requires commitment and change at every level. Policy creates performance expectations that give middle management direction and the ability to address problems. The value of lesbian, gay, bisexual and transgender inclusion is often not understood throughout the company.

Consider the derogatory messages, pervasive in our society, about lesbian, gay, bisexual and transgender individuals. A company must provide training if its employees are to fully understand the value of an equitable work environment. The diversity challenge for middle managers, explains Friend, is that they are pressured between dual ideologies and stakeholders about workplace inclusion: "The middle managers don't have the skills, the time, or the understanding of how to do it. And they have to deal with the backlash. They get an expected backlash from other folks for whom LGBT inclusion is not a priority, and they think that they should not work on it."[103]

"There's the policy and then there's the reality, the culture of the company itself," says Neal Walton, a senior finance officer at Frito

Lay, a division of PepsiCo that is considered exemplary for its commitment to lesbian, gay, bisexual and transgender diversity. "When we first started implementing domestic partner benefits, I think—like at any large company—there was pushback, and there were pockets of pushback. We still get pushback as we try to do training on GLBT issues in some of the more rural areas and in the South.... But it's like a ball that rolls downhill: after a while, things start gathering with it. And the next thing you know, we have non-discrimination policies, we have inclusive training to make sure that LGBT issues are covered, and we sponsor heavily inside the community."[104]

Janet Smith, a senior executive with Citigroup and an outspoken ally at work, provides this overview of making meaningful change: "The first step is getting your policies, practices and benefits in line, and then hopefully hearts follow. I think it's not unlike passing civil rights legislation in the 1960s with the expectation that, over time, you would change the hearts and minds of people, but just changing the law wasn't going to do that. I think it's similar in corporations: The policies help focus an organization on the right thing to do. For example, if I talk to a manager who expresses some concern about our policies, I can say, 'You're entitled to your beliefs. But as a manager, here's what we expect from you from a behavior standpoint.' Over time, the behavior influences the beliefs and creates the culture, but that doesn't happen overnight."

Combining full benefits with an inclusive workplace culture is a combination that places corporations in the best possible competitive position. Employers that provide comprehensive benefits combined with a commitment to an equitable work atmosphere earn the loyalty and dedication of their employees. April Villemaire, who works for IBM, explains, "I have been treated with respect and, on occasion, the company has favored my dignity over others' ignorance. Not once have I felt that I didn't have the company's full support. They are wonderful here, and I hope there are more people as fortunate as me."[105]

David M. Hall

In a company's efforts to create a productive working environment beyond what is measured on most diversity index tools, two fundamental questions must be addressed. First, how does one measure changing the corporate culture? Second, how does one change workplace culture?

Another top financial services company, one that received public recognition for its commitment to LGBT diversity, has taken additional steps to create its own measurement to evaluate its workplace culture. In a company-wide survey, the in-house evaluation allows for self-identification for all minority groups and measures the corporate atmosphere as well as the effectiveness of their Employee Resource Groups. This corporate atmosphere survey is conducted twice each year. The company policy-makers and managers use the data derived from this survey in their effort to serve as an employer-of-choice. While they are troubled that their lesbian, gay, bisexual and transgender employee satisfaction was lower than the general workforce in key baseline categories, they are clearly moving toward equity, as this satisfaction has increased significantly since their 2005 survey. The survey went a step further and attempted to identify what led to employee's low satisfaction. This case study shows a company that is committed not just to a perfect external rating but also to continuing work to transform corporate culture, so that all employees, regardless of sexual orientation or gender identity, feel valued and included.[106]

While most equality effectiveness tools identify valuable criteria, a score truly representative of a company's internal culture should also reflect lesbian, gay, bisexual and transgender employee satisfaction. On a logistical level, measuring all Fortune 500 companies for employee satisfaction through research methods that guarantee anonymity would be overwhelming for any nonprofit organization to attempt. However, within each company, it is essential—and feasible—to include the voices of lesbian, gay, bisexual and transgender employees in assessments of workplace atmosphere and culture. Once the foundations and necessary growth for an equitable work environment are clearly understood, the next challenge is coalition building to create a greater understanding of the need to transform corporate culture.

Senior executive Janet Smith says that while policy development and proper training are key, it is also imperative to develop a network within the organization in order to reach diversity goals: "There are studies that show that training alone is not going to get there. And I do think it takes time, and finding key executives in the organization—LGBT executives who are out, but also allies in senior positions who are willing to help bring the organization along by showing their support—makes a huge difference in making that cultural transition."

This challenge cannot be met without allies. It was heterosexuals who passed the oppressive laws and policies in place during the 1950s. It is heterosexual allies who have instituted many lesbian, gay, bisexual and transgender-friendly workplace policies. Partnership with allies is critical to the restructuring of the work environment in order to reduce and eventually eliminate adversarial experiences and replace them with acceptance and even advocacy.

CHAPTER SEVEN

Strengths and Limitations of an Ally

It is common throughout all of history and across cultures that those
with institutional power resist or even ignore the call for change from
those lacking such power. However, many individuals will respond
differently to this message if they hear it from those who already
have institutional power. If any minority group wants to gain rights
denied to them by the majority, it is helpful, perhaps even necessary,
to have allies who either possess or have access to the institutional
power that affects their lives. Throughout recent American history, in
most civil rights movements religious leaders have played a significant
role in organizing, supporting and articulating the need for change.
Religious advocacy for civil rights includes Martin Luther King's calls
from the pulpit to oppose discrimination through civil disobedience,
and some Catholic parishes urging the liberalization of immigration
laws. Spiritual leaders have raised their powerful voices on behalf of
social justice for a wide variety of minorities. While there are many
spiritual leaders who are fully accepting of lesbian, gay, bisexual and
transgender individuals, many of the high-profile religious leaders
featured by the national media are powerful adversaries. Too often
missing from the national media is the large and diverse population
of clergy who are open and accepting.

There needs to be a clear and high profile source of institutional support for our efforts. People who are lesbian, gay, bisexual or transgender are obviously a critical voice in this effort,
yet there also needs to be inclusion of those who possess a more
pronounced form of influence. Allies must play a significant role

in the struggle for lesbian, gay, bisexual and transgender equity. Allies at work constitute a necessary and powerful source of institutional support.

Thus far this book has examined the implications of language, the so-called culture war, the process of coming out, types of resistance to coming out, and the changing corporate climate as experienced by lesbian, gay, bisexual and transgender employees. I highlighted the importance of developing allies in the workplace. "Allies" in this context usually describes heterosexuals who are open, appreciative, and even advocates for those who have a different sexual orientation or gender identity/expression.

While allies play a valuable and necessary role in this coalition, there are also limitations and potential drawbacks that merit examination. It is important to give consideration to the qualities of an ally. Too often, companies know that they need allies but lack clear criteria for the specific background and skills that an ally should possess. Furthermore, the motivations of an ally are also important to examine. This is necessary not just because it provides different avenues for collaborative work, but also because different motivations will lead to different levels of commitment and evoke a variety of responses from the lesbian, gay, bisexual and transgender coworkers they intend to champion.

Educator and writer Brian McNaught explains the unique and powerful role of allies: "Because gay, lesbian, bisexual and transgender people are invisible, companies have a difficult time identifying them and asking for their guidance, unlike women and people of color. It is much harder to identify gay people and ask them to help you direct your efforts.... Allies are the ones who sometimes start the gay, lesbian, bisexual and transgender resource group. They're invaluable. I tell heterosexuals, 'You need to be aware of your power.' You can say this is an important issue without fearing losing influence."[107]

Allies are indispensable in the work of making genuine change to a more diverse workplace, one with reduced conflict, greater personal acceptance and increased productivity.

It is important to examine the ideal qualities of an active and high-profile ally and to understand that an ally is an educator. While this educator may not offer traditional tutelage in a classroom, every time that lesbian, gay, bisexual and transgender issues are discussed, this person is teaching by how he or she responds or even fails to respond. In fact, most of the teaching may well occur in small groups and one-on-one conversations. The goal is to create as many workplace allies as possible. The Nelson continuum provides a guide for steps to improve workplace conditions. Not every person is going to become an enthusiastic ally or public spokesperson for company diversity. But if a person can be moved from Rejecting Non-Punitive to Qualified Acceptance, that is certainly preferable and a worthy accomplishmet.

The Qualities of an Ally

We need a coalition of as many allies as possible. Though we must be prepared for the fact that they will represent different positions along the Nelson continuum, we also need to have clear criteria for allies who are able to serve as the company face of this alliance. When reviewing the qualities necessary in an ally, envision this person as someone who could provide specific information on lesbian, gay, bisexual and transgender issues in the workplace. There is too much responsibility related to such a high profile role to haphazardly choose someone strictly due to the person's willingness to volunteer.

I have identified seven primary qualities necessary in the attitude and outlook of a high-profile ally [See Figure 7.1].

FIGURE 7.1

Tips for Success: Qualities of an Ally

1. Accept everyone regardless of sexual orientation or gender identity/expression.
2. Be passionate in advocating for an equitable work environment.
3. Possess a strong sense of self.
4. Be culturally competent in lesbian, gay, bisexual and transgender issues.
5. Possess a clear understanding of the legacy of heterosexism and homophobia.
6. Demonstrate model workplace behaviors and attitudes through your everyday words and actions.
7. Be well trained and committed to personal growth.

The first quality is acceptance of everyone regardless of his or her sexual orientation or gender identity/expression. Other people at work need to hear an ally say that no one sexual orientation or gender identity/expression is better than another. The second quality is passion. When working to change the corporate culture, one encounters significant resistance, and these challenges can become exhausting. As a result, an individual who is fully accepting of others but has no particular passion for the cause may find efforts for workplace equity require more energy than he feels inclined to invest. While what I call laissez-faire allies may still provide a valuable perspective around the water cooler, they are unreliable for taking on the difficult challenges of working to change corporate culture, a process that requires the willingness and ability to manage resistance. Coworkers who are fair-minded but passive may endorse change initiated by others, but they do not possess the drive, leadership and educator's zeal necessary for a true ally.

The third quality that allies must possess is a strong sense of self. If someone is involved in an allies program, his colleagues may wonder and even ask whether he, himself, is gay. It is critical that allies care little if such assumptions are made about them. There are some cogent reasons why some people want to be allies, but hesitate to do so, because they do not want to deal with the complications of homophobia. One Fortune 500 employee explained her situation to me, saying, "I want to be an ally, but I am 36 years old and single. I just don't want people to think that I am a lesbian."[108] While her rationale comes out of a motivation to date men, other supposed allies sometimes differentiate themselves from lesbian, gay, bisexual and transgender individuals in a way that undermines the notion that they possess true acceptance. For example, Dr. Richard Friend has observed that sometimes identifying as an ally can sound more like a declaration of heterosexuality: "Often it feels that folks are trying to explain why they're there…. I know the intent is fabulous, but the impact on me is sometimes, 'Some of my best friends are.' It is a need to come out [as a heterosexual ally] so I don't assume that they are gay or lesbian."[109]

The fourth quality is cultural competency. The ally should be able to explain why sexual orientation is innate and not a choice. She should be able to challenge stereotypes and refute them with factual information. There should be a general understanding and deep respect for lesbian, gay, bisexual and transgender cultures. It needs to be stressed that such cultural competency will need to be learned by many allies, so the primary quality should be a willingness to learn as well as sharing fundamental values that allows her, following some diversity training, to articulate culturally competent information in a helpful manner.

The fifth quality allies must possess is a clear understanding of the legacy of heterosexism and homophobia in contemporary

American society. Resistance to equitable treatment in the workplace originates not just from deeply held cultural beliefs that are difficult for many—and impossible for some—to challenge. Addressing lesbian, gay, bisexual and transgender issues in the workplace, even if solely for the sake of workplace productivity, strikes some workers as an attack on their core values. It is important to understand these feelings in order to develop strategies to manage colleagues' resistance. Beyond that, it is also critical that this understanding becomes a vehicle to better understand oneself. The bias that exists in our society can infect everyone, even the most caring and committed allies. Understanding heterosexual privilege is an ongoing and painful journey. Even those who "get it" need to constantly grow, sometimes as a result of emotionally painful insights and experiences.

The sixth quality of an ally is that the person must foster responsible workplace behaviors and attitudes. The leader who is a public ally can have a powerful impact on other heterosexual employees in the workplace. Therefore, it is critical that he or she avoid any hurtful behaviors or comments toward lesbian, gay, bisexual and transgender individuals, because unkind remarks or gestures will convey to coworkers that such behaviors and expressions are acceptable. This person should avoid perpetuating harmful stereotypes, even in what is meant to be good humor, about people who are lesbian, gay, bisexual or transgender. An ally should avoid using the word "gay" in a derogatory way. Beyond what the person should not do, we also need to focus on what an ally should do. Specifically, he or she should take opportunities to advocate for a more inclusive environment and corporate culture. He or she should correct homophobic and heterosexist messages and share accurate information.

Lastly, an ally will be well trained and committed to personal growth. An ally's training should address two areas. First, there should be training to develop cultural competency in lesbian, gay, bisexual and transgender diversity issues. Second, there should be training related to skills development for facilitation and the presentation of information. It is essential that allies also develop strategies for managing resistance from coworkers, because otherwise these challenges can feel like personal attacks and create difficulties for effectively facilitating the program. Training is of paramount importance, as too often people have the best intentions but lack the necessary skills to be effective allies and maximize an ally program's success.

Allies Have Different Motivations

Some allies are motivated by a fundamental belief in equality and social justice, while others are motivated by personal experience with someone who is lesbian, gay, bisexual or transgender. To help illustrate the motivations for becoming an ally, we will analyze a case study that examines motivation for action based on a fundamental belief in justice and equality. The case study helps allies better understand the ways in which they themselves can lead.

Michael works for a Fortune 500 corporation. He has been married for eight years and childless, but he and his wife are trying to have children. His company has a gay and lesbian Employee Resource Group, though he is not entirely sure what an Employee Resource Group may be. Michael describes himself as a live-and-let-live Republican, someone who believes in equality but also wants his taxes lowered and less spending on government programs. He supports gay marriage, though he pays little attention to the issue. Michael has no idea that it is legal to fire someone based on his or her sexual orientation or gender identity/expression.

Michael received an email from his direct supervisor about Judy Shepard coming to speak for a lunch and learn session, and he faintly remembers this story. He recalls that years ago he saw a movie about her son, Matthew Shepard, on cable television. As he read the company email, the details of Matthew's murder brought

David M. Hall

back the distress he felt when he saw the movie. He thought that he was being provided with a remarkable opportunity to hear Matthew's mother speak. Michael attended and found himself moved to tears. Judy spoke not just about her son but also about the status of federal laws. Michael was stunned that laws do not provide the basic protections he had assumed were already in place.

Michael went back to his office and, not realizing that he was already being an ally and advocate, began to tell his coworkers about Judy Shepard's presentation. He shared feeling aghast that the law did not provide basic protections. One of his coworkers, Xin, overheard the conversation and approached him: "Michael, I belong to our LGBT Employee Resource Group. I think that it would mean a lot to our members if you attended our next meeting to talk about your reaction to Judy's presentation."

Xin and Michael spoke at length about the Employee Resource Group and Matthew Shepard's death. Michael knew that people were full of hate, but he had never seriously considered how much injustice might exist in his own community. Michael's view of government was that it should reflect our basic values. In terms of civil rights, Michael could not understand how the law does not protect individuals from bias and discrimination. When he attended the Employee Resource Group meeting, he heard stories of bias that his coworkers experienced each day.

The Employee Resource Group was organizing a group of allies to provide trainings in the workplace. Michael was intrigued. He donates to different organizations and sits on the board of his church, but he had never thought about contributions to his employer beyond the duties of his job. He attended an ally training. After gaining a level of comfort with the curriculum, Michael organized a presentation within his department and co-presented it with Xin. During their presentation, they handed out rainbow flag magnets. Afterwards, Michael found the magnets posted at about 20% of the desks in his department—including those of some high-ranking members of the department. He and Xin then left extra rainbow flag magnets in a common area and found that over the next two weeks the display of magnets increased to about 30% of all desks.

Michael grew closer with Xin, working together in their department and through the Employee Resource Group. Michael's rationale for being an ally quickly expanded to include personal motivations as he became closely connected with a number of lesbian, gay, bisexual and transgender members in his Employee Resource Group. As a result, his two motivations—a belief in equality and then personal regard for people who are lesbian, gay, bisexual and transgender—began to interact with and reinforce each other.

A Different Ally Motivation: Personal Relationships

Many allies find that their initial motivation comes from knowing someone who is lesbian, gay, bisexual or transgender. To help illustrate these concepts, we will examine a case study that involves motivation from this framework.

Growing up, Celia learned and accepted broad cultural and religious messages that homosexuality is a sin against God. A single mom and a diligent worker who never missed church on Sunday, she worked to raise her children with strong moral values and personal integrity. Celia spent her entire life sacrificing for her children. She rented an apartment in an upper middle class neighborhood so that her children, a son and a daughter, could receive an outstanding education from the local school district. Their education motivated Celia to work as hard as possible to afford the rent payments.

Though Celia's formal education consisted of no more than a high school GED, she earned an adequate income. Her children graduated from high school, went to community college and eventually transferred to state schools. Her son, Cesar, became a business major with plans to attend law school. During winter break of his senior year in college, he sat down with his mother one Saturday evening after dinner. With great apprehension, Cesar told his mother that he was bisexual and was generally more attracted to males than to females.

Celia erupted in fury. She told her son that he was confused and demanded that he go to therapy to change his sexual orientation. Cesar was against therapy, because he knew that there was nothing wrong with him, but he wanted to please his mother. While he found the prospect of therapy demeaning, his primary concern at this time was doing all that he could to preserve his relationship with his mother.

He and his mother went to the therapist together. Cesar was soon pleased with therapy, because the experience proved to be a turning point for his mother. The therapist explained to Celia that bisexuality is not a disorder, and then he suggested that they use the meeting to work on Celia and Cesar's mother-son relationship. Since the therapist and Cesar were unwilling to address changing Cesar's sexual orientation, the sessions were used to focus on Celia's and Cesar's feelings. This was when Celia began to process her feelings of blaming herself for not providing a male role model for her son. She thought the fact that he identified as bisexual, rather than gay, meant that he was really a confused heterosexual. The therapist proved helpful in getting her to understand that science shows us that bisexuality, like heterosexuality, is innate and cannot be changed by environment. To describe the process in terms of the Nelson continuum, Celia took gradual steps through therapy, moving from Rejecting Non-Punitive to Qualified Acceptance.

Eventually Cesar took his mother to a meeting at PFLAG, Parents, Families, & Friends of Lesbians and Gays, a place in which Celia could find a support network to help her accept that her son is bisexual. At the point that she entered PFLAG, she was at Qualified Acceptance on the Nelson continuum. By the time she was beginning to reach Full Acceptance, her son was a college graduate and had a promising job with a Fortune 500 company, one that was an industry competitor of Celia's company. He still had plans to attend law school at night during the next semester.

At Celia's next PFLAG meeting, she noticed a sign for their program titled Straight for Equality in the Workplace. She took a closer look and decided to attend the next meeting so that she could better understand Cesar's workplace experiences. Additionally, Celia had been following the news about marriage equality and was hoping that Cesar and his boyfriend would one day be able to provide her with grandchildren. At the same time, she was beginning to understand the obstacles in family law and company policies that denied her son workplace equity.

At the Straight for Equality in the Workplace meeting, Celia learned about the importance of equal benefits and policies. She realized that if her company adopted stronger polices for lesbian, gay, bisexual and transgender employees, her son's company might follow.

Celia had been transformed from a mother who was once at the stage of Rejecting Non-Punitive and was now at the stage of Full Acceptance. Moreover, she was ready to work to change corporate culture with the goal of creating leverage to change rival companies like her son's employer. Her journey led Celia back to doing what she had been doing for the last twenty-three years, working passionately to support and protect her son. At work, she approached her manager and asked how to join the lesbian, gay, bisexual and transgender Employee Resource Group. Her boss did not know, but he connected Celia with the human resources liaison to their department for diversity. She told Celia that while the company had a number of Employee Resource Groups, they were lacking one for lesbian, gay, bisexual and transgender employees. Celia asked, "Then how can we start such a group?"

The human resources officer had been waiting for someone to ask this very question and directed her to Out & Equal's LGBT employee resource groups registry for ideas and best practices for establishing this much-needed Employee Resource Group. Celia had spent her entire career working hard on behalf of her family. It was devotion to creating a safer and more equitable world for her son that drove her to take a leadership role in her company. Celia's advocacy can eventually transform the corporate culture of her employer. Changing her company is the first step to transforming the culture of the industry.

In starting an Employee Resource Group, Celia discovered even more about the workplace environment and family law. As she came to know the details of her colleagues' difficult job experiences, she understood more about the challenges facing her son. Her commitment to equity for her son gave her great empathy for what she regarded as the outrageous challenges faced by her lesbian, gay, bisexual and transgender coworkers.

In the first case study presented here, Michael's becoming an ally was inspired by a speaking event offered by his company's lesbian, gay, bisexual and transgender Employee Resource Group. Celia's commitment rose out of her personal motivation to support her son. In both instances, valuable allies were gained in working for lesbian, gay, bisexual and transgender equity in the workplace. In many situations, however, collaboration with allies is more haphazard than purposeful. Friendly relationships have value, but they prove insufficient to establish reforms that the company or group of employees is committed to for true workplace equity.

It is important to examine the qualities of an ally as well as his or her motivations. Too often, companies know that they need to develop allies but lack clear criteria for the specific background and skills that an ally should possess. The seven qualities of an ally listed in this chapter can guide ally recruitment, assessment and self-assessment.

Furthermore, it is important to consider what motivates an ally. This is necessary not just because it provides different avenues for collaborative work, but also because different motivations will lead to different levels of commitment and so evoke a variety of responses from the lesbian, gay, bisexual and transgender coworkers that allies intend to champion.

Claire Lyons, from the Global Corporate Contributions Department at PepsiCo Foundation, joined her company's Employee Resource Group as an ally. "I understood that there was an opportunity that I could bring some of my joy, my passion, my skills directly to it," she says, "which I knew it would need and could benefit from. But you know, I have many members of my family who are gay. So this isn't something that I'd have to 'get over'… It's just, 'Of course! So let's get on with it. What do you need? How can I help?'… Everyone needs to be able to come to work and be who they are and be respected and be able to contribute in the fullness of their humanness."[110]

Each workplace should make working with allies part of an explicit plan to improve the company atmosphere. While grassroots efforts and one-to-one outreach and education are extremely important, so are company policies and management directives that help encourage and develop allies. Lyons cites her employer's recently introduced Straight for Equality Pledge Tour as a mechanism that set goals for ally recruitment and participation. She describes its purpose: "Let's engage them, let's get them to stand up. Let's help them come out as being allies." Employees are responding by wearing a pledge button, identifying their departments as "safe spaces," or identifying themselves as allies or members of an Employee Resource Group. Not every respondent will go on to take a dynamic role in creating a more inclusive workplace, but with company support and a larger pool of allies, it is likely that a larger percentage will become active.

Tara Bunch, vice president of Global Consumer Support and Service at HP, says, "My experience has been that people aren't necessarily

David M. Hall

not supportive; they just don't know how to *be* supportive. And once you give them an avenue to get involved and engage, once they know people, they can be incredibly supportive." Describing her company's new mentoring program, which matched straight executives interested in being allies with gay and transgender employees interested in being mentored, Bunch continues, "I think this will energize a lot of people to get involved, to be allies, to learn how they can help. And I think it will also help LGBT employees to feel like they have access: people they can call, people they can influence. Together, I think it will give us an opportunity to move more of the progress forward that we want in the company, with more people working in the same direction."[111]

CHAPTER EIGHT

Over the Corporate Rainbow: Working with Allies to Change Workplace Culture

Allies are a necessary part in lesbian, gay, bisexual and transgender workplace inclusion, but too often there is a lack of a plan or understanding of the best ways to utilize them. In many cases, allies are welcomed and even sought in absence of a concrete plan for the best approach for collaboration. This is the equivalent of a baseball coach knowing that he needs a shortstop but not being entirely sure what a shortstop does or where he plays on the field. To effectively identify concrete steps in which allies' voices and skills can be utilized, it is necessary to better understand the qualities of an ally and the motivation of an ally. This chapter will present possible ways in which we can collaborate with allies for leadership and as well as ways in which we can plan advancement toward workplace equiy.

Psychologist Glenda Russell, senior research associate at the Institute for Gay and Lesbian Strategic Studies, has conducted research on allies that identifies specific roadblocks that stop or slow the development of ally advocacy. She has also analyzed the characteristics and conditions that enable or motivate advocacy. The following are barriers identified by Russell that prohibit allies from working for lesbian, gay, bisexual and transgender equity:

1. Time.
2. Money.
3. Fear of not being accepted.
4. Closed lesbian, gay, bisexual and transgender cliques.
5. Having motives questioned.

6. Fear of coming across as homophobic.
7. Lack of opportunity.[112]

Money and time are significant obstacles that many lesbian, gay, bisexual and transgender individuals and their Employee Resource Groups have limited ability to change. For many, the most effective approach may be to help company leadership to recognize the value in having an employee participate in an Employee Resource Group. As a result, individuals could see Employee Resource Group work as part of what will help their careers rather than as something that takes time away from other pressing demands that they may consider the sole route to bonuses and promotion.

FIGURE 8.1

Tips for Success: Working with Allies

1. **Develop strategies to avoid the major obstacles to ally involvement identified by Glenda Russell:** time; money; fear of not being accepted; closed lesbian, gay, bisexual and transgender cliques; having motives questioned; fear of coming across as homophobic; and lack of opportunity.
2. **Develop strategies for allies' involvement:** having an opportunity, being asked to help; being seen; having a sense of collaboration; being free to ask questions; receiving support for dealing with their own homophobia; and being supported by the ally's own family.
3. **Identify examples of basic support, moderate support and advocacy.** Allies should examine what type of support they are in the best position to offer and develop concrete ideas for what they can do.

Fear of not being accepted can be a significant barrier to ally participation. As noted in the previous chapter, one woman feared that she would be assumed to be a lesbian, and she did not want that misperception to reduce her dating opportunities. Other potential allies may fear that their peers will mock them for their advocacy. Typically, there are specific departments in any company in which it is more difficult to find allies and a support network. There are also interpersonal issues that can inhibit advocacy. For example, an employee who seeks a promotion and knows that her boss opposes a company diversity initiative may feel it is in her best interest to distance herself from the diversity efforts as much as possible.

Potential allies may perceive that a group is reserved solely for lesbian, gay, bisexual and transgender participants. If ally partnership is valued, it is important to convey that message clearly. Additionally, people may worry that their motives will be questioned and they will be seen as perhaps insincere in their efforts. It is critical that allies who are valued partners are fully aware of the degree to which their energy and support is appreciated, especially if they are getting negative feedback in other circles for their dedication and commitment to lesbian, gay, bisexual and transgender equity.

Fear of appearing homophobic is a significant obstacle for many allies and potential allies. They are concerned that they will say something that will strike others as heterosexist or homophobic. Indeed, it is a real possibility that this will occur while growing and learning. It is vital that lesbian, gay, bisexual and transgender work colleagues assure allies and potential allies that it is understood that people make mistakes and sometimes simply need further education.

Author and educator Brian McNaught is well aware of this anxiety on the part of allies and potential allies. He offers the following advice: "Trust your instincts. Trust that your heart is in the right place. Don't worry about making a mistake. Gay people will pick-up that you care about them—if that is your motivation. If it is to find out how to improve the working conditions, don't worry about saying something that's possibly offensive, because people will consider the source."[113]

Lack of opportunity, according to Glenda Russell, is a major roadblock to becoming an ally. Most allies are unaware that they are welcome to play a leadership role. Indeed, allies play a vital role for invisible minorities that would be highly inappropriate with other minority groups. When was the last time you saw a white person co-chair a racial minority Employee Resource Group? Many allies assume that they cannot and should not play a leadership role related to lesbian, gay, bisexual and transgender issues. It is crucial that they come to understand that opportunities exist for participation and leadership.

Dr. Richard Friend offers an insightful perspective on the value of an allies program: "For me, when we start to think of allies, I broaden it. All of us need allies regardless of who we are in the world. All of us should be allies for other people and should be allies around the issue of inclusion."[114] Indeed, any successful community or larger society consists of allies, human beings supporting each other so that we develop an increased sense of community and loyalty. In every facet of life, these relationships help us to excel in our efforts. In fact, a strong motivation and a sensible argument to advance is that allies help create a work community that reflects our basic human-ity. This is a perspective that conveys the need and value of allies, to which virtually everyone should be able to relate.

As an ally who works with passion and intensity on behalf of lesbian, gay, bisexual and transgender social justice, I still find many of these barriers arise for me. I am constantly fearful that my het-erosexual privilege will appear offensive to some who are denied the same rights. Because of this fear I regularly seek feedback to ensure that my message is coming across as intended. I have found repeatedly that these concerns are virtually always just my own and that my lesbian, gay, bisexual and transgender colleagues and friends understand my intended meaning and regard my advocacy positively. I have reached the conclusion that I need to live with these concerns as long as I work as an ally. Additionally, I have reached a corresponding conclusion: the concerns that lead to seeking feedback are helpful and necessary in my growth and work as an ally.

Factors That Help Develop Allies

Dr. Glenda Russell has identified internal and external factors that help someone become an ally. As this chapter is focused on working with allies, it is particularly valuable to focus on the external factors involved:

1. Having an opportunity.
2. Understanding the reality of homophobia and heterosexism.
3. Being asked to help.
4. Being seen: feedback about their work.
5. Having a sense of collaboration.
6. Being free to be unsure, to ask questions.
7. Receiving support for dealing with their own homophobia.
8. Being supported by the ally's own family.[115]

Many of these criteria have been examined in a variety of contexts in these pages. However, one significant area for further examination lies in having an opportunity. Employee Resource Groups, lesbian, gay, bisexual, transgender individuals and allies themselves need to be clear in reaching out to other allies, in letting them know that they have a role to play in support of these efforts. Some people will not consider participating, let alone leading, unless they are asked to do so. Requesting that they do so can lead, at a minimum, to an increased understanding of efforts to transform the workplace culture. Additionally, this can generate new leadership that improves

Employee Resource Group efficacy in influencing the corporate culture so that it becomes increasingly reflective of the values of workplace equity.

Psychologist Glenda Russell notes that allies need to see that the issue of equity also includes them: "Gay people assume that being an ally is all about them. It's not. The allies I trust most in this world don't see it as all about gay people. They see it as an issue that they have a stake in."[116] She cites the story of an ally in Colorado who worked on the Supreme Court case of *Romer v. Evans*. She explained that he was involved in the case not because of commitment to lesbian, gay, bisexual and transgender individuals but, instead, due to his interest as an attorney in litigating important issues. Additionally, a valued mentor invited him to work on the case. This demonstrates the power of inviting people to become allies.[117]

Steps toward Progress

Reflecting on the 5 P's for Workplace Equity outlined in Chapter 2, we need to explore how we **Progress**. What specific actions need to be taken to transform corporate culture into an equitable environment for lesbian, gay, bisexual and transgender employees? There is no cookie-cutter approach that fits every corporation, and to act as if a single plan of action exists would be pointless. However, there are distinct steps to take whenever changes in employment policy and workplace culture are desired. Virtually every allies program should include four primary stages: identifying the areas that need to be addressed, identifying allies, providing training, and identifying strategies and activities to implement workplace changes.

The first necessary step, identifying the area(s) that need to be addressed, often occurs through a lesbian, gay, bisexual and transgender Employee Resource Group, a human resources department, a diversity office, allies, or a combination of these groups. If your employer has no Employee Resource Group, a term commonly abbreviated as ERG, and you are not a part of the other groups, you might form your own group to examine changing the workplace culture. The needs vary tremendously among corporate workplaces. For example, because at this time there are no federal and few state laws protecting workers from being fired based on sexual orientation or gender identity/expression, a workplace that has not developed its own inclusive policies will likely start with this issue. Where employers offer workplace protection but no domestic partner benefits, employees are likely to focus on benefits. In contrast, companies that receive a perfect LGBT diversity ratings are likely to examine ways in which they can better reach genuine equality and continue to make improvements in the corporate culture.

Develop a Diverse Network of Allies

Identifying the area(s) to be addressed should create additional criteria regarding the types of allies one hopes to work with. It is valuable to collaborate with a diverse group of allies. Diversity is valuable regarding race, religion, gender, age, disability, sexual orientation, and gender identity/expression. Equally important is diversity in the positions allies hold within the corporation, both in terms of rank and in the variety of departments. For example, if your primary issue of concern is domestic partner benefits, then you will want to consider whose voice speaks most powerfully to that specific issue.

It is also important to be careful about the types of assumptions that are commonly made about potential allies. Individuals cannot be easily categorized, and it is counter-productive to predetermine who will be adversarial to lesbian, gay, bisexual and transgender individuals based on political ideology, religious beliefs, socio-economic status, or any other arbitrary measure. Conversely, coworkers cannot be assumed to be supportive based on their general worldview, faith or politics. Allies are just as diverse as any other group.

Glenda Russell notes that there are "unexpected allies," whom she describes as unexpected not just to her but also to themselves. These are individuals who come from a background in which they learned that homosexuality is wrong, but they find themselves so motivated by their opposition to hatred and bigotry that they become leading allies. She points to examples that she finds among Mormons, Catholics and fundamentalist Christians.[118]

Additionally, I cannot begin to count the number of times I have met someone of a relatively conservative political nature who I later learn is accepting of homosexuality. For example, I worked with a conservative Republican for whom I had great respect and felt a strong professional rapport. He never voted for Democrats and had a passionate belief in Republican policies and their rationale. I assumed that I knew his views on homosexuality, since I could not identify a single issue in which he diverged from Republican Party orthodoxy. Then, in a personal conversation, he said to me, "The one issue that I disagree with Republicans about is homosexuality. I just don't get how it fits into our overall philosophy." Clearly, my assumptions had been unfair to my colleague. However, they were also damaging to the very cause of equity that I work to champion. Here was an ally whom I had not even considered approaching. He was someone who had a level of credibility with a group at work to which I lacked easy access. He was ready to support our efforts and offer his leadership whenever we asked. However, I wasted precious years assuming that I should not even bother to inquire about his support.

Allies often turn up in unexpected places, and expectations can actually limit effective networking. A gay employee at Quaker Oats says an open-minded approach has been essential for building relationships across the spectrum: "I think you should never assume that you don't have an ally in the person sitting next to you. I think our biggest lessons learned were to actually reach out to our other

Employee Resource Groups.... It's a simple thing to attend another ERG's event. And when you can show that support, it usually comes back to you as well.

"It's also the same for individuals," he adds. "You never know and can't assume that the person who may seem very conservative isn't necessarily an ally. And you have to give them that opportunity and really reach out to them in a safe and friendly way. That, I think, can motivate folks to want to learn more—oftentimes, more about you as a person, which of course is a great bridge to learning more about us as a community."[119]

Discounting potential support is one problem. Another is assuming that alliances will be immediate or automatically understood. Amanda Simpson, a chief engineer at Raytheon Missile Systems and a national spokesperson on gender identity issues, recommends taking an open-minded, educational approach with all potential allies: "We talk about reaching out into the straight community for allies. But within our company, it was very important to reach out to the gay and lesbian community for allies and to educate... I've actually done workshops on the history of transgender issues and the media—and how [being transgender] was always portrayed as an extreme form of being gay or lesbian. And people within the gay or lesbian community haven't really understood the transgender part."[120]

Concrete Steps to Take

In this next step, individuals should feel comfortable seeking allies and asking for their support. At the same time, it is critical to think carefully about the messages that are being used to inspire them. Start by reaching out to individuals who have said something supportive in the past. You can also make a brief comment during a department meeting that you are reaching out to allies. Finally, ask people individually if they have an interest in serving as allies. Sometimes individuals are waiting to be asked. If you are a mentor, reach out to the person you mentor. If you are being mentored, reach out to your mentor. Ask your boss if he or she would like to be supportive.

When talking with allies, remind them that there are many things that each individual can do to help create a more equitable work environment for all employees regardless of sexual orientation and gender identity/expression. Here are some concrete steps that can be taken to help ensure workplace equity:

Basic Support

- Make a point of using inclusive words such as "partner" or "spouse" that do not assume that everyone with whom you are speaking is in a heterosexual relationship.
- Place a rainbow flag sticker or button—or literature from your company's lesbian, gay, bisexual and transgender Employee Resource Group—in your office area.
- Stay up-to-date on lesbian, gay, bisexual and transgender workplace issues, and share workplace-appropriate informational emails about lesbian, gay, bisexual and transgender issues and individuals.
- Talk with your colleagues about the things that you do in support of lesbian, gay, bisexual and transgender workplace equality.
- Attend ongoing lesbian, gay, bisexual and transgender diversity training and programs at work and in your community.
- Listen for—and avoid—making assumptions about a person's sexual orientation or gender identity.

Moderate Support

- Correct anti-gay jokes or slurs.
- Correct the use of the word "gay" when it is used in a derogatory way.

- Support equitable treatment in company policies and enforcement of those policies for all employees regardless of sexual orientation or gender identity/expression.
- Attend lesbian, gay, bisexual and transgender Employee Resource Group events at your company and invite other allies to join you.
- Offer to review employment and product collateral (forms, advertisements, etc.) at your company to suggest ways that language and images used can be more inclusive.

Advocacy

- Join your Employee Resource Group/Diversity Council.
- Become a workplace trainer on lesbian, gay, bisexual and transgender issues and look for opportunities to speak publicly about your journey as an ally.
- Volunteer to work with your company's training department to review or develop a training program in your workplace.
- Encourage your company to be an advocate for local, state, and national legislation that supports lesbian, gay, bisexual and transgender workplace equality.

Note: Handout 8.1, which appears later in this chapter, provides these guidelines in a one-page format that is easy to copy and distribute at work.

Collaborate with as many allies as possible to develop support. However, make sure to pay particular attention to the allies that you ask to lead.

When speaking with an ally, do not just ask them to lead. They are likely to have lots of questions and some anxiety about championing this cause. People do not want to make a mistake or accidentally appear bigoted. I would recommend making the following messages clear to individuals about the growth that they will go through as allies: It is okay to ask questions. It is okay to make mistakes. Remember that what you are doing is for the good of everyone. A closer examination of each of these areas is critical.

What You Can Do for Workplace Equity

DR. DAVID M. HALL There are many things that each individual can do to help create a more equitable work environment for all employees regardless of sexual orientation and gender identity/expression. Here are some concrete steps that you can take to help ensure workplace equity.

Basic Support
- Make a point of using inclusive words such as "partner" or "spouse" that do not assume that everyone with whom you are speaking is in a heterosexual relationship.
- Place a rainbow flag sticker or button—or literature from your company's lesbian, gay, bisexual and transgender Employee Resource Group—in your office area.
- Stay up-to-date on lesbian, gay, bisexual and transgender workplace issues, and share workplace-appropriate informational emails about lesbian, gay, bisexual and transgender issues and individuals.
- Talk with your colleagues about the things that you do in support of lesbian, gay, bisexual and transgender workplace equality.
- Attend ongoing lesbian, gay, bisexual and transgender diversity training and programs at work and in your community.
- Listen for—and avoid—making assumptions about a person's sexual orientation or gender identity.

Moderate Support
- Correct anti-gay jokes or slurs.
- Correct the use of the word "gay" when it is used in a derogatory way.

- Support equitable treatment in company policies and enforcement of those policies for all employees regardless of sexual orientation or gender identity/expression.
- Attend lesbian, gay, bisexual and transgender Employee Resource Group events at your company and invite other allies to join you.
- Offer to review employment and product collateral (forms, advertisements, etc.) at your company to suggest ways that language and images used can be more inclusive.

Advocacy
- Join your Employee Resource Group/Diversity Council.
- Become a workplace trainer on lesbian, gay, bisexual and transgender issues and look for opportunities to speak publicly about your journey as an ally.
- Volunteer to work with your company's training department to review or develop a training program in your workplace.
- Encourage your company to be an advocate for local, state, and national legislation that supports lesbian, gay, bisexual and transgender workplace equality.

David M. Hall

Developing Expertise and Making Mistakes along the Way

First, allies need to know that it is okay to ask questions. Allies are not immune to stereotypes or to misunderstanding the diversity among lesbian, gay, bisexual, and transgender individuals' issues and priorities. Allies need to feel comfortable seeking clarification of what they do not understand. One elected official who was supportive of lesbian, gay, bisexual and transgender individuals asked me privately: "Why do they walk around parades wearing nothing but tight underwear? I just don't get it. If I wanted to be accepted by the mainstream, I wouldn't present myself like that." This is an ally who is a leader in his state, but who felt the need to ask questions in a private forum so that he would not be judged publicly as perpetuating stereotypes. His comfort in asking allowed me to address his observation: It is a common stereotype, not representative of the entire community, but nonetheless an expression of identity for some; it is as an accepted part of the diverse lesbian, gay, bisexual and transgender community.

Second, allies need to understand that it is okay to make mistakes. I cannot count the number of allies in work settings that I have heard talk about "alternative lifestyles." Such language is hurtful, as lesbian, gay, bisexual and transgender lifestyles are little different from heterosexual lifestyles, yet such language is never used to describe heterosexuals based solely on their sexuality. I find that when allies use language that pushes a button for their colleagues working for lesbian, gay, bisexual and transgender equity, educating them about why a particular word or expression is hurtful is enough to get them to change their language. Mistakes are likely to be common.

Heterosexism and homophobia, as already detailed in this book, have deep roots in our society and shape our language and perspectives more than we realize. Even a motivated, well-meaning ally has a great deal to learn and personally overcome. In fact, those of us who spend much of our professional careers as allies learn more and more each day. However, just the fear of sounding prejudiced is enough to keep some allies from speaking up or putting themselves forward. That fear of making mistakes must be countered, because it is too costly to our efforts to achieve workplace equality.

Lastly, allies need to remember that their work is not charity but an investment in the kind of world we want to live in. Homophobia and heterosexism exact a price from all of us. That is what interferes with workplace productivity for millions of people across America. Many employees put a great deal of energy into hiding their identities as lesbian, gay, bisexual, or transgender people instead of investing that energy in productive solutions for their company.

Formal Components of Ally Training

The next step involves training allies. In order to have truly effective allies, extensive training is necessary. If allies are going to make presentations to others within the workplace, they need to develop a deep understanding of issues related to being lesbian, gay, bisexual or transgender. Preparation for teaching and facilitation is required, as are strategies for managing resistance.

The presentation of content should be included with development of teaching and facilitation skills. If instructional training does not occur, most programs will develop a strong preference toward lecture, which will be disadvantageous to the overall goals. The lecture format has the following weaknesses:

1. Each passing minute is correlated with a decrease in attention of the learners.
2. The primary information gained will be lower-level learning of factual information.

3. Different needs for information are neglected or ignored.
4. Most learners give poor reviews to this style.[121]

Most people prefer to utilize the lecture method despite its ineffectiveness. This is understandable, because lecturing is the easiest model to be utilized by an instructor, especially when skills in active training are lacking.

Evaluations of the knowledge gained during a training session show that the information is likely to be forgotten within just a few hours if it is only obtained in a lecture format. Mel Silberman, an author and coach to seminar leaders, reports research demonstrating the techniques that provide enhanced learning. Quality active training should feature trainers who:

1. State the information in their own words.
2. Give examples of their information.
3. Recognize their subject matter in various guises and circumstances.
4. See connections between their topic and other facts or ideas.
5. Make use of their information in a variety of ways.
6. Foresee some of the consequences of implementing the training.
7. State the opposite or converse of the information that is shared.[122]

There are three domains to address in an effective active training program: affective, cognitive and behavioral. The first domain to be addressed is the affective one, in which we examine personal feelings, values and beliefs. This should include reflections on our own upbringing and the ways in which that has influenced our beliefs today. It should also be noted that corporations that already address lesbian, gay, bisexual and transgender issues through trainings and guest speakers tend to do the best job in this specific domain. While such speakers and sessions can be compelling, they are likely to have a limited impact in developing the change necessary to have a truly equitable work environment.

The second domain is the area of cognitive development. This domain should provide the trainees with information related to history, the challenges of coming out, and the impact of the larger society on workplace productivity. This domain covers a wide range of information, and allies should not be expected to provide expertise on every aspect of lesbian, gay, bisexual and transgender issues. However, allies should be able to cite at least some of the scientific evidence that demonstrates that people are born with a certain sexual orientation. They should be able to explain the ways in which bigotry and bias keep lesbian, gay, bisexual and transgender employees from fully participating in the workplace. They should be able to make a compelling case for workplace inclusion.

The third domain is behavioral or skills development. This is the least likely domain to be covered in typical workplace trainings and speaker events. However, this domain is critical if we are to create a work environment that truly honors equality regardless of sexual orientation or gender identity/expression. The area of skills development encompasses more than just presentation and facilitation skills. It also includes having a deeper understanding of the skills development we want to foster throughout the workplace. For example, in training human resources professionals, it is valuable to spend time examining and developing their language skills, so that when these staff members discuss issues with lesbian, gay, bisexual or transgender individuals, they do not use language that leaves employees feeling left out or poorly understood.

The last area of training following skills development is managing resistance. It is likely that you will be challenged when working to change corporate culture. When challenged, it is common to feel defensive. However, defending yourself and, even worse, counterattacking, can get you off track, taking you off message and onto the turf of the person challenging you.

Remember that not everyone will agree with you. Your conversations about LGBT diversity and equality will be far more productive, though they may present far more personal challenges for you, if you allow people to speak honestly. The process requires correcting inaccurate information but also permitting the expression of views that you do not hold and perhaps even find hurtful. Of all of the skills necessary to develop, this can be the most difficult and exhausting. Allies and diversity trainers often feel great passion for this work. To hear contrary views can be hurtful and feel like a personal attack. However, we need to remember that oppositional remarks are rarely personal attacks but, instead, show individuals grappling with their own personal value systems and how they relate to efforts to change corporate culture. In contrast to resistance, being an ally provides an opportunity to find allies of your own, those who admire and support your efforts in creating a more inclusive work environment. I have found working as an ally results in far more joy and rewards than challenges.

This chapter is intended to serve as a framework to improve the recruitment of allies and to identify steps that an ally can take. Creating opportunities for ally leadership and collaboration requires identifying obstacles to becoming an ally and the factors that help people invest their time as allies. A variety of skills and resources are necessary for success. Training allies to lead, facilitate and cope with resistance are necessary to maximize their impact on the corporate culture.

CHAPTER NINE

Where Do We Go from Here?

The workplace situation is suboptimal for many lesbian, gay, bisexual and transgender workers. We need to fix that. This book aims to be not just a source of information but also a call to action to create a more inclusive working environment. To initiate change, work with an existing group or start one dedicated to lesbian, gay, bisexual and transgender inclusion. The goal is to devise a strategy and activities to address the needs identified for your specific workplace. These activities ultimately change corporate culture.

This chapter provides activities to conduct in a training to get you started on working toward greater workplace equity. If you have an Employee Resource Group or work in a Human Resources or Diversity department, utilize these activities with your colleagues. If you have a passion for change but do not have an ERG or work in those departments, gather a group of like-minded individuals and get started with them.

While many diversity trainers are reluctant to publish materials they have developed as part of their professional services, I feel it is critical that *Allies at Work* offer not just general information but also a first, concrete step for changing your corporate culture. Provided here is a facilitation activity for use in the workplace. It includes guidelines for workshop preparation and facilitation, along with worksheets to use in the meeting. By outlining a structured activity—and making the structure visible in these pages—the author aims to assist readers in initiating a process that produces increased workplace equality.

Title of Training

Toward Workplace Equality: Step One

Rationale

In order for companies to be competitive in the 21st century economy, it is necessary for corporate culture to become inclusive of all employees regardless of their sexual orientation or gender identity/expression. This section identifies specific steps that need to be taken to allow a company to increase its competitive advantage as an employer-of-choice and, if applicable, as a company that lesbian, gay, bisexual and transgender consumers choose to purchase from.

In our efforts to create these changes, we need to collaborate with allies to move toward equity at work. A concrete plan needs to be developed that identifies our goals and examines the crucial role that allies can play in fostering that change.

Length of Time

90–120 minutes

Objectives

As a result of this session, participants will be able to…

1. Identify specific issues impacting lesbian, gay, bisexual and transgender employees that need to be addressed in the workplace.
2. Examine concrete ways in which allies can play a role in working for that change.

Materials

- See Handout 9.1. Provide one copy for each participant.
- Small circle stickers.
- Flip chart.

- Markers.
- Masking tape.

Procedure

1. Divide participants into groups of no more than four individuals per group.
2. Explain to participants that we are going to examine specific issues that we feel are priorities to be addressed within our workplace.
3. Instruct them to complete worksheet 9.1 "Toward Workplace Equality."
4. Allow participants a minimum of 20 minutes to discuss the issues raised in the worksheet.
5. As a large group, list on the flip chart all of the issues raised related to employees, consumers, and supplier diversity. Have each group present their plan for how they think each issue should be addressed. (Plans reflect their answers to questions 5 through 8 on Handout 9.1).
6. After each plan is presented, ask others the following questions:
   - How would change on this issue be in the best interest of our company?
   - What are the strengths of this approach?
   - What are some different approaches that we could consider?
7. Discuss which issue(s) of all of those brainstormed need to be addressed in this specific workplace.
8. Provide each individual with 3-5 circle stickers. (Each individual should get the same number of stickers—decide how many votes you would like each member to have). Instruct them to place a sticker next to the issues that they feel are most critical to address. They can vote for as many issues as

they have stickers. However, they cannot vote for any issue more than once, although they can choose to withhold some of their votes in case they feel particularly strongly about one issue.

9. In looking at the results, record the issues in order of importance, based on the majority's votes. When discussing this list, keep in mind the following:

    • There is no minimum or maximum number of issues that should be addressed.

    • The goals must be realistic for your workplace. In most cases, if you do not have a non-discrimination policy, it may be strategically ineffective to start with bereavement leave. The first policy affects everyone year-round, while the second one benefits fewer employees and only at intervals.

    • It is helpful if a common theme can be identified for why it is in the best interest of the company to address more than one issue.

10. Ask the group the following questions:

    • Which of these top-rated issues do we want to address?

    • Which of these top-rated issues is it most practical to address?

    • What is our message that connects these issues?

11. Set up another meeting specifically to examine working with allies and adversaries. The second meeting will also be a forum for individuals to take specific responsibilities for working on this initiative.

Toward Workplace Equality

1. What are some of the most important issues facing our company regarding workplace diversity related to lesbian, gay, bisexual and transgender employees?

    A. _____
    _____
    _____

    B. _____
    _____
    _____

    C. _____
    _____
    _____

2. What are some of the most important issues facing our company regarding lesbian, gay, bisexual and transgender consumers?

    A. _____
    _____
    _____

    B. _____
    _____
    _____

    C. _____
    _____
    _____

3. What are some of the most important issues facing our company regarding supplier diversity related to lesbian, gay, bisexual and transgender companies?

    A. _____
    _____
    _____

B. _____

_____

_____

C. _____

_____

_____

4. Of all of these issues, what three issues are the most important issues to address?

   A. _____

   _____

   _____

   B. _____

   _____

   _____

   C. _____

   _____

   _____

Choose one of the three issues from #4 and answer the following questions:

5. What groups (e.g., departments, other ERGs) or individuals will be supportive of our goals, and how do we motivate them to actively support our efforts?

6. How do we energize supportive groups and individuals to support us and be active?

7. What groups or individuals may be resistant or opposed to our efforts?

8. What can we do to win their support or at least neutralize their opposition?

This activity should be the start of a detailed and ongoing effort to develop strategy and activities to implement workplace changes, an effort that seeks to fundamentally change a company—for the company's own sake. This process for change allows a corporate community to consider the implications of the lack of equity and its impact on workplace productivity.

The activity suggested here is only the start of the process. If a group goes through the actual implementation of questions 5 through 8, the results can lead to a considerable investment of time and mental energy devoted to advocacy. While the initiatives, work settings and outcomes vary, those who come together to implement the strategy and activities will experience compelling results. As a diversity seminar leader, I have seen that when participants complete the strategy and exercises, the number of participants who believe that they can influence policy triples. Just participating in this program strengthens advocates' resolve. The belief in one's ability to change policy is invaluable in the ongoing efforts to create change. Utilizing this program may very well be the start of changing policy. However, regardless of the impact on specific policies, the process of clarifying goals, objectives and roles will strengthen the group's confidence in its ability to create change in the workplace. The long-term impact will be a stronger group leading the drive toward workplace equity.

The Good, the Bad and the Beautiful

The early chapters of this book examine language and politics, in order to provide a framework for workplace equity. Subsequent chapters focus on coming out and offer personal stories and examples to help allies better understand some of the challenges faced by a non-visible minority. Next, a historical perspective establishes the immensity of the task of changing corporate culture. The next chapters focus on the power of allies in fostering diversity and creating an all-inclusive worksite. Finally, the last chapter provides materials to guide an initial group meeting to plan for changing corporate culture. These materials support the process of moving from *talking* to *doing*. While success is certainly not guaranteed, people are unlikely to achieve success unless they take action, which will benefit not just individuals but also the corporation.

The reality is that the challenges for creating true workplace equity are considerable. Establishing equity can be so difficult that in many companies, there may be more failed attempts than successes. It can be infuriating to fight for simple fairness and lose. Keep in mind that working for change has never been easy. Consider that it took over 70 years after the Seneca Falls Women's Rights Convention for American women to win the right to vote—a civil right that African American women and men in many Southern states had to continue to fight to establish until the 1960s.

Those who work to create change in their corporate culture sometimes do so at great risk. They may be seen as agitators, and this can impact their career trajectory. At a minimum, they are focusing on changing business operations in a way that will cause discomfort for a number of their colleagues. This points to the importance of establishing policy, the company framework that supports managers and employees in their conversations, work situations or struggles with prejudiced or antagonistic colleagues. While it may be uncomfortable to take on the responsibility of reform, remember that any significant changes in American society—from the birth of this nation through the present—have required taking risks. In fact, our history books dedicate little space to those who seek only safety and comfort.

Today's advocates already benefit from the hard work carried out during the first wave of reform, by pioneers who risked so much more. Our efforts to create and improve workplace inclusion are almost expected by many large corporations, due to the work, policy and successful models already established.

Additionally, for those who have been active in any cause, there are few feelings more elating than creating meaningful change that moves us toward equity. Tremendous satisfaction and meaning can be derived from helping form a community, and ultimately a world, that more closely reflects our humanity. These victories themselves inspire further hard work to address the next objective in creating an equitable workplace environment.

Neal Walton, a senior finance manager at Frito Lay, a company which has courted lesbian, gay, bisexual and transgender customers through advertising campaigns, corporate giving and other programs, gives this overview of his company's progress over the last decade: "We've come light-years since we originally announced domestic partner benefits. It's not even thought of anymore as being a big issue at all. And I think that it's just like knocking down dominoes: you start and you push that one thing down, and then something else comes along, and the next thing. We certainly have policies in place. There's no doubt about that. And the questions have come up... 'Okay, we're there on the policies, but how do we change the culture? How do we keep doing that?' And that's something you do day by day, that's not something you do like knocking down a domino. You change one heart and one mind, one person at a time."[123]

"People understanding diversity, especially LGBT diversity, has to do with the human connection," says Marcelo Roman, an IBM executive who leads the company's global learning delivery outsourcing services in 68 countries. "We announced domestic partner benefits in 2005 for all of the countries where IBM does business, including Latin America. To accomplish that, we had to find allies in those countries. We found country general managers and other executives that we were able to connect with through some personal stories, and they became our ambassadors, they became our allies. And the country general managers are so committed that they're saying, 'What can I do to make sure that the people in my organization feel okay to come out?'

"So telling the story and making that human connection between an LGBT employee and an ally or a decision maker or a human resources executive makes a tremendous difference… The human connection is very, very important for us to drive any of our initiatives forward."[124]

Those who read this book already possess enough passion to educate themselves on this issue. The next step is establishing the path toward equity. That requires ongoing education and advocacy. It requires a level of energy, understanding and patience that on some days will be difficult if not nearly impossible to find. On other days, it will come quite easily. However, one day this era will be written about as history. It is up to us to decide on which side of history we will stand. Much has already been accomplished by pioneering gay and transgender employees who risked their own jobs and incomes to advocate for equality. They have dedicated so much, because more was at stake than just improving their own individual workplace experiences. For many of us, work is an essential part of who we are. Lesbian, gay, bisexual and transgender individuals who are in the closet often isolate themselves as a form of protection from the bigotry and hatred that exists in the mainstream.

Our work for lesbian, gay, bisexual and transgender workplace equity improves people's life experience by allowing them to take down the barriers that protect, isolate and limit them in the workforce. We are creating a workplace that reflects our humanity, the belief that every individual should feel a valued member of the team. An atmosphere of respect for diversity is what we owe to those who dedicate so very much to a company's advancement. Dedication to workplace equity for all employees safeguards the efficacy and livelihood of our loved ones and colleagues while strengthening our companies, community and nation.

Resources and Organizations

941 Action
941action.org

Atticus Circle
www.atticuscircle.org

CenterLink: The Community of LGBT Centers
1325 Massachusetts Ave. NW, Suite 700
Washington, DC 20005
www.lgbtcenters.org

David M. Hall Associates, LLC
Silver Lake Executive Campus
41 University Drive, Suite 400
Newtown, PA 18940
www.davidmhall.com

Equality Federation
2069A Mission Street
San Francisco, CA 94110
www.equalityfederation.org

Gay Men's Health Crisis
The Tisch Building
119 West 24th Street
New York, NY 10011
www.gmhc.org

Gay & Lesbian Alliance Against Defamation
5455 Wilshire Boulevard, #1500
Los Angeles, CA 90036
www.glaad.org

Gay, Lesbian and Straight Education Network
90 Broad Street, 2nd Floor
New York, NY 10004
www.glsen.org

Gay-Straight Alliance Network
1550 Bryant Street, Suite 800
San Francisco, CA 94103
www.gsanetwork.org

Human Rights Campaign
1640 Rhode Island Ave. NW
Washington, DC 20036-3278
www.hrc.org

Lambda Legal
120 Wall Street, Suite 1500
New York, NY 10005-3904
www.lambdalegal.org

David M. Hall

**National Center for
Lesbian Rights**
870 Market Street, Suite 370
San Francisco, CA 94102
www.nclrights.org

**National Center for
Transgender Equality**
1325 Massachusetts Ave. NW,
Suite 700
Washington, DC 20005
www.nctequality.org

**National Gay and Lesbian
Chamber of Commerce**
1612 U Street NW, Suite 408
Washington, DC 20009
www.nglcc.org

**National Gay and Lesbian
Task Force**
1325 Massachusetts Ave. NW,
Suite 600
Washington, DC 20005
www.thetaskforce.org

**Out & Equal Workplace
Advocates**
155 Sansome Street, Suite 450
San Francisco, CA 94104
www.outandequal.org

Out for Work
1325 Massachusetts Ave. NW
Suite 700
Washington, DC 20005
www.outforwork.com

**Parents, Families, & Friends
of Lesbians and Gays**
1726 M Street NW, Suite 400
Washington, DC 20036
www.pflag.org

Pride at Work
815 16th Street NW
Washington, DC 20006
www.prideatwork.org

**San Francisco
AIDS Foundation**
995 Market Street, Suite 200
San Francisco, CA 94103
www.sfaf.org

Who Am I
A PricewaterhouseCoopers LLC
Diversity Resource
"Who Am I" is an example
of how one company promotes
being an ally.
www.pwc.com/diversity

Endnotes

INTRODUCTION

1   Gay Lesbian and Straight Education Network (2008, April 2). Press release: "GLSEN's Day of Silence honors the memory of Lawrence King."

2   Stacy, Mitch (2007, March 24). "City manager who wanted sex change fired." *Saturday Star*.

3   Human Rights Campaign (2008). "Don't ask, don't tell, don't pursue, don't harass."

4   Planet Out (2008, April 2). "Senator Kennedy lobbies for ENDA protection without trans protections."

CHAPTER ONE

5   Miller, Neil (2006). *Out of the past: Gay and lesbian history from 1869 to the present*. New York: Alyson Books.

6   Intersex Society of North America (2008). "What is intersex?"

7   McNaught, Brian (2008, May 29). Personal interview.

8   *Ibid*.

9   Green, Eli (2008, May 31). Personal interview.

10   Sestak, Joseph (2008, May 27). Interview via email correspondence.

11   Thomas, Jacqueline (2003, April 3). "When co-workers decided I was gay," Human Rights Campaign.

CHAPTER TWO

12   Human Rights Campaign (2007, Nov. 7). "U.S. House takes historic step by passing the Employment Non-Discrimination Act."

13   Planet Out (2008, April 2). "Senator Kennedy lobbies for ENDA protection without trans protections."

14   Out & Equal (2007, Sept. 11). "Significant majority of all adult Americans believe it is unfair that federal law allows employers to fire someone because they are gay or lesbian."

15   *Ibid*.

16   Human Rights Campaign (2008, March 31). "Statewide employment laws and policies."

17   National Lesbian & Gay Journalists Association (2008). "Domestic partner benefits overview."

18   *Ibid.*
19   Gunther, M. (2006, Nov. 30). "Queer Inc." *CNNMoney.*
20   Musback, Tom (2004, Sept. 17). "Anti-gay groups boycott Procter & Gamble." *PlanetOut Network.*
21   Human Rights Campaign (2009). *Corporate equality index: A report on lesbian, gay, bisexual and transgender equality in corporate America.*
22   Berry, Selisse (2008, May 30). Personal interview.
23   Gunther, M. (2006, Nov. 30). "Queer Inc." *CNNMoney.*
24   *Ibid.*
25   *Ibid.*
26   Out & Equal (2007, Sept.). "Understanding the lesbian, gay, bisexual and transgender perspective in the workplace."
27   Human Rights Campaign (2007, Sept. 17). "New report finds unprecedented growth in employer policies for lesbian, gay, bisexual and transgender workers."
28   Human Rights Campaign (2009). Corporate equality index: A report on lesbian, gay, bisexual and transgender equality in corporate America; Human Rights Campaign (2009, Sept. 2). "Number of companies with top rating for lesbian, gay, bisexual, and transgender jumps by one-third."
29   Human Rights Campaign (2007, Aug. 25). "GLBT equality at the Fortune 500."
30   Nika, Greg (2008). Out & Equal 2008 Summit interviews.
31   Wolf, Adam (2008). Out & Equal 2008 Summit interviews.
32   Anonymous (2008. April 15). Personal interview: Chicago, IL.
33   Friedman. T. (2007). *The world is flat.* New York: Picador.
34   Gunther, M. (2006, Nov. 30). "Queer Inc." *CNNMoney.*
35   *Ibid.*
36   Out & Equal (2007, Sept. 11). "Significant majority of all adult Americans believe it is unfair that federal law allows employers to fire someone because they are gay or lesbian."
37   *Ibid.*
38   Servicemembers Legal Defense Network (2006, Dec. 13). "Latest news."
39   Gunther, M. (2006, Nov. 30). "Queer Inc." *CNNMoney.*
40   Out & Equal (2007, Sept. 11). "Significant majority of all adult Americans believe it is unfair that federal law allows employers to fire someone because they are gay or lesbian."
41   Out & Equal (2006, Oct. 10). "Seven out of ten heterosexuals today know someone who is gay."
42   Out & Equal (2006, Oct. 10). "In the lesbian, gay, bisexual and transgender workplace."
43   *Ibid.*
44   Out & Equal (2007, Sept. 11). "Significant majority of all adult Americans believe it is unfair that federal law allows employees to fire someone because they are gay or lesbian."

45 Gunther, M. (2006, Nov. 30). "Queer Inc." *CNNMoney.*
46 Human Rights Campaign (2008, Feb. 15). "Relationship recognition in the U.S."
47 Lindenberger, Michael (2008, June 14). "California's gay marriage rush." *Time.*
48 Human Rights Campaign (2005, Oct. 13). "Alabama custody and visitation law."
49 Human Rights Campaign (2007, March 10). "Kentucky custody and visitation law."
50 Lambda Legal (2008). "Adoption and parenting."

CHAPTER THREE

51 Cass, Vivian (1979). "Homosexual identity formation: A theoretical model." *Journal of Homosexuality.*
52 Belcher, David (2008, May 7). "Preacher's pride before the fall." *The Herald.*
53 Rotello, Gabriel (1997, April 1). "The enemy within—homophobia among gay men." *The Advocate.*
54 Berry, Selisse (2008, May 30). Personal interview.
55 Out & Equal (2006, Oct. 10). "In the lesbian, gay, bisexual and transgender workplace."
56 Anonymous (2008, May 9). Personal correspondence.

CHAPTER FOUR

57 Nelson, James B. (1978). *An approach to sexuality and Christian theology.* Minneapolis: Augsburg Publishing House.
58 Helfand, L. (2007, March 1). "Stanton: Abrupt firing a surprise." *St. Petersburg Times.*
59 Reinhard, Brent (2008, June 1). Personal interview.
60 Berry, Selisse (2008, May 30). Personal interview.
61 Reinhard, Brent (2008, June 1). Personal interview.
62 Smith, Janet (2008). Out & Equal 2008 Summit interviews.
63 Eagan, Chris (2008, June 2). Personal interview.
64 Schlenoff, Marla (2008). Out & Equal 2008 Summit interviews.

CHAPTER FIVE

65 United States Senate (1950). "Employment of homosexuals and other sex perverts in government."
66 Human Rights Campaign (2008). "Corporate equality index: 2008 statements from employers that rated 100 percent."
67 Peiss, Kathy, editor (2002). "Massachusetts colony's laws on sexual offenses, 1641-1660." *Major problems in the history of American sexuality.* Boston: Houghton Mifflin Company.

68   Miller, Neil, editor (2006). "The United States in World War II." *Out of the past*. New York: Alyson Books.
69   *Ibid*.
70   Peiss, Kathy, editor (2002). "The U.S. Senate investigates 'sex perverts' in government, 1950." *Major problems in the history of American sexuality*. Boston: Houghton Mifflin Company.
71   *Ibid*.
72   *Ibid*.
73   *Ibid*.
74   Miller, Neil, editor (2006). "The United States in World War II." *Out of the past*. New York: Alyson Books.
75   Miller, Neil, editor (2006). "The age of McCarthy." *Out of the past*. New York: Alyson Books.
76   *Ibid*.
77   *Ibid*.
78   Scalia, Antonin (2003). Dissenting. "Lawrence v. Texas." Supreme Court of the United States.
79   Human Rights Campaign (2004). "Key dates in the quest for gay marriage."
80   CNN.com (1996, September 10). "Anti gay marriage act clears Congress."
81   Amestoy, Jeffrey (1999). "Stan Baker, et al. v. State of Vermont, et al.". *Supreme Court of Vermont*.
82   Human Rights Campaign (2004). "Key dates in the quest for gay marriage."
83   CNN.com (2004, May 17). "Same sex couples ready to make history in Massachusetts."
84   Human Rights Campaign (2004). "Key dates in the quest for gay marriage."
85   Sokolove, Michael (2005, May 22). "The believer." *New York Times Magazine*.
86   Senate of the United States (2005, January 24). "Proposing an amendment to the Constitution relating to marriage."
87   Steele, Bruce (2004, December 7). "Now what?" *Advocate*.

CHAPTER 6
88   Out & Equal (2007). "Fifteen steps to an out & equal work environment."
89   Human Rights Campaign (2008). "Corporate equality index: 2008 statements from employers that rated 100 percent."
90   *Ibid*.
91   *Ibid*.
92   *Ibid*.
93   *Ibid*.
94   Human Rights Campaign Foundation (2007). *The state of the workplace for gay, lesbian, bisexual and transgender Americans*.

95 Halleman, James (2008). "Interview with James Halleman." *Human Rights Campaign.*

96 *Ibid.*

97 Anonymous (2007, August 7). Personal interview.

98 Young, Louise (2008). Out & Equal 2008 Summit interviews.

99 Eagan, Chris (2008, June 2). Personal interview.

100 Human Rights Campaign Foundation (2007). *The state of the workplace for gay, lesbian, bisexual, and transgender Americans.*

101 Friend, Richard (2008, June 11). Personal interview.

102 *Ibid.*

103 *Ibid.*

104 Walton, Neal (2008). Out & Equal 2008 Summit interviews.

105 Villemaire, April Elizabeth (2008). "Transitioning at work." *Human Rights Campaign.*

106 Reinhard, Brent (2007, November 7). "Measuring employee resource group effectiveness and employee satisfaction."

CHAPTER 7

107 McNaught, Brian (2008, May 29). Personal interview.

108 Anonymous (2008, June 20). Personal interview.

109 Friend, Richard (2008, June 11). Personal interview.

110 Lyons, Claire (2008). Out & Equal 2008 Summit interviews.

111 Bunch, Tara (2008). Out & Equal 2008 Summit interviews.

CHAPTER 8

112 Russell, Glenda (2007). "Allies: Who, why, and how?"

113 McNaught, Brian (2008, May 29). Personal interview.

114 Friend, Richard (2008, June 11). Personal interview.

115 Russell, Glenda (2007). "Allies: Who, why, and how?"

116 Russell, Glenda (2008, June 27). Personal interview.

117 *Ibid.*

118 Russell, Glenda (2008, June 27). Personal interview.

119 Anonymous (2008). Out & Equal 2008 Summit interviews.

120 Simpson, Amanda (2008). Out & Equal 2008 Summit interviews.

121 Silberman, Mel (1998). *Active training: A handbook for techniques, designs, case examples, and tips.* New York: Josey-Bass/Pfeiffer.

122 *Ibid.*

CCONCLUSION

123 Walton, Neal (2008). Out & Equal 2008 Summit interviews.

124 Roman, Marcelo (2008). Out & Equal 2008 Summit interviews.

Index

Allies at Work

Index

A

acceptance, quality of, 104
acronyms and abbreviations, 3, 5–6
active training programs, 130–131
Adams, Henry, 40–41
adopting children, 30, 31–32
advocacy, 125, 127
affective domain, 130–131
Alaska, same-sex couples in, 82
allies
  advocacy by, 125, 127
  basic support by, 124, 127
  concrete steps for, 123–127
  definition of, xvii, xxxi
  developing expertise as, 128–129
  diverse network of, 121–123
  evolving journey of, xviii
  factors in becoming, 119–120
  help provided by, 11–12
  importance of, xiii–xvi, 101–103
  language issues and, 2, 128–129
  mistakes made by, 128–129
  moderate support by, 124–125, 127
  motivations of, 102, 107–112
  obstacles to involvement by, 115–118
  opinions on inclusive work environments, 26–29
  personal qualities of, 103–107
  resources and organizations for, 145–146
  responding to coming out as, 58, 75
  steps toward progress by, 120–121
  training of, 106–107, 129–132
  unexpected, 122
  working with, 115–132
alphabet soup abbreviation, 3, 5
American Civil Liberties Union (ACLU), 81
American Family Association (AFA), 11, 21
American Psychiatric Association (APA), xx–xxi
Arizona, same-sex couples in, 84
Association for Gender Research, Education, Action and Academics (AGREAA), 6
author's personal journey, xvii–xxxi
aversion therapy programs, 39–40

B

Baillie, Patricia, 25
Ballmer, Steve, 23
behavioral domain, 131
Bell, Hayward, 19, 91
benefits
  domestic partner, 16–17, 93
  workplace, 15–17, 88, 93
Berry, Selisse, xvi, 18, 44, 74
bisexual employees. *See* LGBT employees; sexual orientation
Bunch, Tara, 113–114
Bush, George W., 14

C

California, same-sex couples in, 29–30, 84

Index **153**

David M. Hall

pride in the workplace, 26
Procter & Gamble, 17–18, 19
procurement of LGBT employees, 25
productivity in the workplace
    family law and, 33
    improving, xvii–xviii, 12, 23–26
professional development, 88
progress for LGBT employees,
    24–25, 28, 120
protection of LGBT employees,
    23–24

Q

Quaker Oats, 122
Qualified Acceptance responses,
    66–68
    case study on, 67–68
    explanation of, 66–67
qualities of allies, 103–107
queer, use of word, 6

R

Raytheon, 19, 91, 94, 123
Reinhard, Brent, 65–66
Rejecting Non-Punitive responses,
    61–66
    case study on, 65–66
    explanation of, 61–62
Rejecting Punitive responses, 59–61
    case study on, 62–65
    explanation of, 59–61
religious leaders, 101
Republican policies, 122
resistance management, 131–132
resources and organizations, 145–146
risk taking, 142
Roe, John, 30–31
Roman, Marcelo, 90, 143
Romer v. Evans (1996), 120
Russell, Glenda, 115–116, 118, 120, 122

S

same-sex couples
    corporate rights for, 82
    marriage controversy for, 16

parents as, xxvi, 29, 30–33
state laws on, 29–30, 32–33, 82–85
See also domestic partners
Santorum, Rick, 83
Scalia, Antonin, 81
Schipper, Brian, 91
Schlenoff, Marla, 74–75
Schwarzenegger, Arnold, 84
self-protection, 61
Seneca Falls Women's Rights
    Convention, 141
sense of self, 105
Sestak, Joseph, 7
sexual orientation
    appreciating differences in, xvii
    custody rights and, 32
    educating students about, xx–xxi,
        xxii–xxiv
    federal and state laws on, 13–17,
        82–85
    legacy of discrimination based on,
        78–81, 105–106
    stages of coming out, 37
    See also gender identity/expression
Shepard, Judy, 107–108
Shepard, Matthew, 8, 107, 108
Shields, Mark, 28
Silberman, Mel, 130
Simpson, Amanda, 123
skills development, 131
Smith, Janet, 71, 97, 99
Solmonese, Joe, 20
spiritual leaders, 101
SprintNextel Corporation, 91
Stanton, Steve, xxv, 60–61
state law
    banning marriage equality, 84
    LGBT adoption and, 31–33
    same-sex couples and, 29–30,
        82–85
    workplace equity and, 15
    See also federal law
Steps to an Out & Equal Workplace,
    87–89
Straight for Equality Pledge Tour, 113

158 Index